This Wine of Peace,

This Wine of Laughter

THIS WINE OF PEACE,
THIS WINE OF LAUGHTER

A Complete Anthology of Japan's Earliest Songs

Translated by Donald Philippi

with Photographs by Kuzunishi Sōsei

A Mushinsha Limited Book

Published by Grossman Publishers

Distributed in Japan by
CHARLES E. TUTTLE CO., Inc.
Suido 1-chome, 2-6, Bunkyo-ku
Tokyo, Japan

First published in the United States of America
in 1968 by
GROSSMAN PUBLISHERS, Inc.
125 A East 19th Street
New York, N. Y. 10003

Designed and produced by Mushinsha Limited, IRM/Rosei Bldg., 4, Higashi Azabu
1-chome, Minato-ku, Tokyo, Japan. Copyright in Japan, 1968, by Mushinsha Ltd. All
rights reserved. Printed in Japan.
First Edition, 1968.
Library of Congress Catalog Card No. 68-27534

Preface

The keen interest which the modern Western reader feels in the verse, as well as the art, of peoples with widely divergent cultural backgrounds, particularly in that of ancient, preliterate, and primitive societies, cannot be explained entirely by his taste for the exotic.

It is true, of course, that the type of appreciation we feel for ancient Egyptian or Mesopotamian verse, for American Indian songs, or for classical Chinese and Japanese poetry, is of an entirely different order than that which we give to the literatures of peoples of the Western orbit. It is further true that these literatures are rich in elements strange and new to the Western reader, who is sometimes baffled by what he finds in them. But, under the superficial exotic over-layer, is there not some elemental basic core from which the modern reader can gain authentic literary nourishment?

Ancient societies, folk societies, primitive and pre-literate societies, although mutually divergent in many aspects of their cultures, tend to agree in basing their approach to reality on myth and magic. This mytho-magical atmosphere is, of course, the womb from which their poetry springs, and, as has often been suggested, the very stuff that fine poetry is made of. The poetry of such societies, for all its naïveté and unadorned directness, is very often endowed with an elemental power which more sophisticated poetry cannot attain.

Preliterate, ancient poetry is communal, rather than individual; ceremonial, rather than personal; and the powerful diction and striking symbolism of this poetry seldom fails to produce a deep impression on modern readers.

Ancient Japan—the Japan which had not as yet felt strong cultural influences from the Asiatic mainland, the Japan of the pre-Nara (–710 A.D.) and Nara (710–794 A.D.) periods—also possessed such a poetry, which in its main outlines fulfills all the conditions mentioned above for ancient, pre-literate poetry.

It is unfortunate that ancient Japanese verse has until now been introduced only partially and imperfectly, and has been thought of importance only as foreshadowing the poetry of the *Manyōshū*, the first great anthology of Japanese literary poetry. Although in numbers far inferior to the *Manyōshū*, it will be seen that the body of pre-*Manyōshū* poetry possesses its own unique literary values and gives us a rare glimpse into the inner life of a fascinating people.

What can a Western reader expect to find of interest in ancient Japanese verse?

First there is an animated, lively diction peculiar to only this period of Japanese verse. Although at times a trifle long-winded, the ancient songs are never pedantic, never allusive, and never dreary. Their irrepressible vitality, their displays of technical virtuosity, and their natural freshness are never-ending sources of wonder.

Besides the technical aspects, far more than one might expect and hope, these songs put us into intimate contact with the inner workings of the ancient Japanese heart, giving us extremely frank and revealing glimpses of these far-away people. There are many curiosities awaiting the reader in this body of verse—the completely sensual nature of the love depicted here (songs 48–49), the odd songs about menstrual blood (songs 222–223), the ribald political satire (songs 210–212), the all-pervasive concreteness of the imagery and the wide use of figurative language.

The extreme plasticity and the total lack of abstractions have reminded one film theorist of the techniques of the motion picture.* In these songs, as in the film, everything moves by means of visual images; associations, even the most tenuous, are played on to the full.

As to the literary value of this ancient Japanese verse, opinions and tastes differ. Tachibana Moribe, a Japanese scholar of the Edo period, numbered some of the ancient songs as among the best of all Japanese verse of any period. They will, on the other hand, be disappointing for those who prefer the refined and sophisticated in poetry. But certainly nothing else will satisfy those with a taste for the primitive, and it is no coincidence that a number of modern *tanka*† poets have gone back to them for inspiration.

The reader of a translation of these songs is both blessed and cursed. He is blessed because of the ease with which he can penetrate to the essential meanings of the songs—an ease not shared by the modern Japanese reader, to whom the original texts mean very little. He is cursed because much of the primitive flavor is inevitably lost in translation.

In translating these songs, I have attempted to make them enjoyable reading. I feel that these ancient songs have a certain affinity to modern ways of poetic expression and have a contribution to make in enriching modern literature. I hope that they will not be regarded as mere literary relics or curiosities, but as lively, animated songs sung by extremely human people living in a remote historical period—people living in an atmosphere singularly amenable to poetic expression.

* Tahei Imamura, *Eiga no honshitsu*, p. 79–81.
† Traditional Japanese 31-syllable poem.

Contents

Introduction

The 313 songs in this volume are the entire body of pre-Heian Japanese verse, known collectively as "ancient Japanese songs" *(Nihon jōdai kayō)*.

They include the oldest existing specimens of Japanese verse, as well as all extant Japanese verse of the Nara and pre-Nara periods (i.e., before the year 794 A.D., when the capital was moved to what is now Kyōto), exclusive of the *Manyōshū*, the great anthology of literary poetry.

Their antiquity entitles them to the term "ancient," although "archaic" might be a more appropriate term. The word "primitive" has also been used to characterize them; but there is little in common in them with the verse of tribes on a primitive technological level, nor was the age in which they were produced a primitive one. Ancient Japan had attained a high civilization, was ruled by a well-developed central government, had diplomatic relations with foreign countries, an army, laws, a system of writing of sorts—in short, was by no means on the primitive level.

The verse is called "songs" rather than "poems" because it is felt that the former term reflects more accurately what they actually were. There is every reason to believe that the majority were actually sung and handed down orally for some time before being reduced to writing. The only exceptions, as will be pointed out, are some literary songs contemporary with the *Manyōshū*, such as those recorded in the work called *Kakyō Hyōshiki* (these I have given at the end of this volume).

DOCUMENTARY SOURCES AND NUMBER OF SONGS

The number of the ancient songs varies according to the person counting them. I have omitted two songs (numbers 112 and 255 in Takeda's *Zoku Manyōshū*) the texts of which were so corrupt that I could make little sense of them. Counting these two omitted songs, I end up with a total of 315, exactly the same as in Takeda's *Zoku Manyōshū*—although my method of counting is not exactly the same. Accurate numbering is almost impossible because of the large number of variant versions found in different documents.

The songs are culled from a large number of source documents—over 20, to be exact. The majority come from the two ancient historical books, the *Kojiki* and *Nihon Shoki*, which contain, respectively, some 113 and 128 songs. Because many of the songs duplicate each other in part or whole, the actual number of single songs (not counting their variants or duplicates) boils down to only about 175—which is well over half of the entire collection. Thus, the songs from these two works, known collectively as the *Kiki kayō*, are the basic part of the whole body of verse.

The *Kojiki*, the earliest work written in the Japanese language, was completed in 712 A.D. It chronicles the history of Japan from its mythological beginnings in the Field of High Heaven until the death of Empress Suiko in 628 A.D. A treasure-trove of myth, legend, songs, and historical facts, the *Kojiki* is written in Chinese characters which are read in Japanese. The English translation of the *Kojiki* by Basil Hall Chamberlain, now long out of print, is based upon the pre-modern scholarship of Motoöri Norinaga and Tachibana Moribe and is extremely inadequate by modern scholarly standards. In particular, the translation of the songs is inferior and unpoetic.

The *Nihon Shoki* is a much more voluminous historical work, completed in 720 A.D. It is less literary in emphasis than the *Kojiki*, and is written in pure Chinese in imitation of the style of the Chinese dynastic histories. Its narrative, beginning with mythological accounts, goes through the reign of Empress Jitō, who abdicated in 697 A.D. The songs in the *Nihon Shoki* often overlap with those in the *Kojiki*, but those recorded in the later years of its narrative include many so-called *waza-uta*, or popular songs to which the compilers attached a prophetic significance. These *waza-uta*, which are not found in the *Kojiki*, make up a peculiar and fascinating group of their own and are found, although in lesser numbers, also in other ancient books. The English translation of the *Nihon Shoki* (under the alternate title *Nihongi*) by W. G. Aston is far superior to Chamberlain's translation of the *Kojiki*, but neither is thoroughly satisfactory by modern standards. The translations of the songs are better than those of Chamberlain.

Besides the songs of the *Kojiki* and *Nihon Shoki*, there is a large body of around 140 songs found scattered in a number of other documentary sources. There has been an unfortunate tendency in Japan to overlook these other pre-Heian songs and to treat the *Kiki kayō* as the sole representatives of the verse of this period; foreign scholars have hardly even been aware of this body of verse, practically none of which has ever been introduced or translated into foreign languages. In the present work, this entire body of verse is given together with all of the *Kiki kayō*.

The *Kakyō Hyōshiki*, compiled in 772 A.D. by Fujiwara-no-Hamanari (724–790 A.D.), is the earliest book of Japanese poetry criticism. Besides being an example of early critical literature, it also contains the texts of many poems, 25 of which I have included in this volume. Because the verse quoted in the *Kakyō Hyōshiki* is largely literary poetry akin to the poetry of the *Manyōshū*, I have grouped it all in a separate place at the end of the "Miscellaneous" section. This verse really does not belong with the ancient songs and has been included here largely for the sake of completeness.

The *Kinkafu* ("Notes for *Koto* Songs") is an early Heian collection of words and *koto** notation for some 21 songs, some of which overlap with songs in the *Kojiki* and *Nihon Shoki*. The book exists in only one manuscript copy, which was not known at all until it was discovered in 1924 by Dr. Nobutsuna Sasaki in the library of the Konoye family. The songs contained in this book are believed to be *ō-uta*, or ceremonial songs sung at Court on various occasions in the year. Since this book is the only example of musical notation of any of the ancient Japanese songs, it is of the utmost value in all research into the musical aspects of the subject.

The famous song tablet preserved at Yakushi-ji Temple in Nara bears 21 songs (only 20 of which are completely legible) inscribed in antique characters; these songs are presented here in a group (songs 123–142) and are explained in detail on p. 91.

The ancient geographical works known collectively as *Fudoki* contain some 23 songs known to date from the pre-Heian period. Most of these works survive only as fragments quoted in other works, but all are extremely important source materials for the Nara and pre-Nara periods.

The *Shoku Nihongi*, the official historical work which takes up where the *Nihon Shoki* leaves off, covers the period 697–791 A.D. and was completed in 797. It contains 8 songs.

The *Jōgū Shōtoku Hōō Taisetsu* is a biography of Prince Shōtoku (died 621) believed to ante-date the *Kojiki*; it contains 4 songs. Several other songs connected with Prince Shōtoku are contained in the *Shōtoku Taishi Ryakuden* and the *Jōgū Shōtoku Taishi Den Hoketsu Ki*, other ancient biographical works of Prince Shōtoku.

The *Owari no Kuni Atsuta Dai-jingū Engi* (Story of the Origin of the Atsuta Grand Shrine in the Land of Owari) was compiled in the Heian period but includes 4 Nara period songs which had been handed down locally.

The *Kōtai Jingū Gishiki Chō* (Book of Ceremonies of the Inner Shrine at Ise), compiled in 804 A.D., contains two ceremonial songs of the shrine dating from the Nara period.

The *Honchō Getsurei* (Monthly Orders of the Court) was a Heian work describing court ceremonies; one Nara period song is found in a quotation from it in the *Nenchū Gyōji Hishō* (Secret Compilation of Ceremonies Throughout the Year).

The *Nippon-koku Gempō Zen-aku Ryōiki* (abbreviated as *Nippon Ryōiki* or *Ryōiki*), is a collection of ancient stories of wonders compiled by Buddhist priests in the

---

* Japanese horizontal harp.

Heian period. It contains some 9 Nara period songs, including some interesting songs of political satire.

There is one song (song 285) written on the back of an old document preserved in the Shōsō-in Treasure House at Nara.

The *Tōdaiji Yōroku*, written in the early 12th century, contains 4 songs dating from the Nara period.

Besides these, this volume contains one song from the *Kagura-uta*, two from the *Kokin Waka-shū*, one from the *Saibara*, one from the *Tosa Nikki*, and two from the historical work *Nihon Kōki*. All of the above songs are, of course, believed to date from the pre-Heian period.*

AUTHORSHIP AND DATE OF THE ANCIENT SONGS

The verse contained in this volume differs from most collections of verse in that nearly every song is accompanied by a prose narrative specifying the historical occasion on which it was sung. If it was not a song sung by a historical or legendary character, then it was a song performed on a certain occasion in the Imperial Court or at some local celebration. Judging by outward appearances alone, we would be forced to conclude that this is a collection of purely occasional verse.

However, when we examine the verse more closely, it becomes clear that there are a number of ways in which a song can be connected with its narrative. Some of these are as follows:

1. A song may be unmistakably and irrevocably connected with its own particular narrative and may, by its very wording, be applicable to no other case. Many of the songs of recent date can be safely accepted as being the works of their attributed authors (or of their amanuenses), and the content of some songs identifies them as having unmistakably come into being in connection with their narratives. Many of the songs in the section entitled "Narrative Songs" (songs 241–274) fall into this category.

2. A song may, on the other hand, have no connection whatever with its narrative, and may apparently have been inserted in it only by mistake or because of some geographical or other superficial similarity with the circumstances of the narrative.

3. A song may both fit its narrative and also be susceptible of a more general application.

4. A song possessing an entirely independent origin may have been skillfully edited to fit the narrative—the proper nouns changed, the diction altered to apply to the situation at hand. It is not unusual for one song to be attributed to more

---

* Though the works in which they occur may be of a later date.

than one narrative—sometimes none of which is appropriate to the words of the song text.

Thus, it is obvious that there are various circumstances under which songs became connected with their narratives and that no single theory will unfailingly apply to all cases.

We must recognize the wisdom of considering each song—whenever at all possible—in two lights. First, the song should be cut free from its narrative and appreciated entirely by itself as an independent piece of verse. By comparison with other ancient Japanese verse and by an analysis of the text, one can frequently determine that the song had a meaning quite different from that attributed to it in its narrative. Second, the song should be replaced into its traditional context in order to discover why it was that the compilers of the ancient books should have regarded such-and-such a song as being an appropriate utterance of such-and-such a character in such-and-such a situation. The way in which a song is woven into a narrative frequently provides us with important clues about the history of a song, its functions, and the role it played in the life of the ancient Japanese.

As to the chronology of the songs, I must say that the vast majority—about nine-tenths—of them are identified as belonging to a definite historical period; quite often the exact year, even the day and month, on which a certain song was first sung is given.

However, the notorious unreliability of the earlier reaches of the Japanese historical works makes it utterly impossible to accept uncritically any historical dates before the reign of Empress Suiko (592–628 A.D.). Only about one-fourth of the extant songs are dated from the period after the year 592—around 84 songs; and only about one-eighth, around 44 songs, date from the Nara period (710–794 A.D.).

Thus, the vast majority of the songs are attributed to the pre-Suiko period, a period in which legend is interwoven with historical fact.

Although the *Manyōshū* is an anthology of poems of the Nara period, it also contains a few—around 11, to be exact—which are dated before the Suiko period, and over 430 pre-Nara poems. Thus, there is a certain overlapping of historical period between the later of the ancient songs and the earlier of the *Manyōshū* poems. In fact, there are some instances of the same item being included—usually in a slightly different version—in both the *Manyōshū* and one of the older documents.

With regard to the large body of pre-Suiko texts, we have nothing but our imagination to go on in attempting to date any of them. Some Japanese theorists attempt to determine the relative antiquity of some songs by the "early" or "late" appearance of the metrical structure and diction; as there is no way of knowing, however, which of the songs have been tampered with by later scribes and compilers, this type of analysis can result in nothing more than a vague, general conjecture.

Since the majority of these songs can be safely presumed to have been transmitted orally for comparatively long periods before their reduction to writing, it is only to be expected that they should have extremely complex backgrounds; the existence of the many variants and of extremely similar expressions in different songs should suffice to show conclusively that these songs have passed through many hands—or rather mouths—during the process of transmission.

GRAPHIC AND PHONETIC COMPOSITION OF THE ANCIENT SONGS

The vast majority of the songs are written entirely with *Manyō-gana*, i.e., Chinese characters used phonetically to represent the sounds of the ancient Japanese language. In this style of writing, the ideographic principle is abandoned, and each character represents one Japanese syllable. These very *Manyō-gana* later assumed abbreviated forms and developed into the Japanese syllabary script, the *kana*.

Besides the songs written in this phonetic script, there are a very few songs written, in the manner of most of the verse of the *Manyōshū*, in a mixture of *Manyō-gana* and Chinese characters used ideographically to represent the meanings of Japanese words.

The ancient songs are written in the oldest known Japanese, and phonetically and grammatically this archaic language differs greatly from modern Japanese.

Perhaps the most surprising fact about ancient Japanese phonology is the existence of eight vowels (modern Japanese has only five: *a, i, u, e,* and *o*). The three additional vowels of ancient Japanese are transcribed by Japanese phonologists as *ï, ë,* and *ö*. The exact phonetic values of these vowels are not certain; however, the *ö* is believed to be something like German *ö*. During the late Nara and early Heian periods, these three vowels gradually became amalgamated with *i, e,* and *o*; but in the texts of the ancient songs and in the *Manyōshū*, separate sets of *Manyō-gana* are consistently used to distinguish between the two sets of vowels: *i, e, o* and *ï, ë, ö*. (Of course, transcribed *e* is always to be read with full value, never silent.)

As for consonants, there existed the syllables *ye, we, wo,* and *wi,* no longer found in the language. *Zi* and *di* were separate sounds; modern *sa* and *so* seem to have been pronounced *tsa* and *tso; tsu* and *zu* were pronounced *tu,* and *du; shi* and *chi* were pronounced *si* and *ti.* It is certain that the sound *h* did not exist in the language of the Nara period; the modern Japanese sound *h/f* was, in remote antiquity, a *p,* which by the Nara period had changed to an *f.*

In most cases I have transliterated the Japanese words in the translated texts approximately in their modern pronunciation. In order to give the reader an idea of the divergence between the ancient and modern readings, I reproduce here the text of song 1 in both ancient and modern transliterations. The ancient transliteration is on the left.

Ama tsakaru	*Ama sakaru*
Fina-tu-me no	*Hina-tsu-me no*
I-watarasu seto	*I-watarasu seto*
Isi-kafa kata-futi	*Ishi-kawa kata-fuchi*
Kata-futi ni	*Kata-fuchi ni*
Ami fari watasi	*Ami hari watashi*
Më rö yösi ni	*Me ro yoshi ni*
Yosi yori ko ne	*Yoshi yori ko ne*
Isi-kafa kata-futi	*Ishi-kawa kata-fuchi*

MUSIC OF THE ANCIENT SONGS

In dealing with this body of verse, it is always necessary to remember that these were not poems written to appeal to the eye as literary works, but songs which were actually sung and may have been handed down orally for long periods of time before being written down.

Unfortunately, we can say little more about how these songs were actually sung than we can say about how the songs of the Chinese *Shih Ching* or the Psalms were originally sung.

The melodies of all of the ancient songs are lost. The only clues which we have are provided by the *Kinkafu*, which contains complete melodic notation of a kind for only two of its 21 songs. The *Kinkafu*, however, does provide information on the tempo and rhythm of the songs it records.

We possess many musical names of the songs. Some 34 of these names appear in connection with about 73 of the songs. Some of these names are taken from the words of the songs, some seem to refer to the manner of singing, and some refer to the occasions on which the songs were performed. Other names refer to the community in which the songs were handed down. In the notes I have indicated these musical names.

It is certain that many—or most—of the song texts have been abbreviated and made to conform to a preconceived metrical pattern. It is possible that the songs, when actually sung, were much longer and had many repetitions, refrains, and additional words and syllables. Sometimes the same song appears in two different documentary sources; in one source it will be shorn of all unnecessary elements and will conform nicely to some metrical pattern, but in the other source it will contain refrains, repetitions, and additional words. The *Kinkafu*, in fact, does give two versions: first, an abbreviated version containing the essential words only; and second, the words in the notation, which faithfully record all the repetitions, prolongations, and refrains. Frequently there are discrepancies between the two versions. Thus, it is always safe to suspect that the words in the ancient documents are mere skeleton texts, which were much elaborated in actual performance. In translating the songs, I have usually chosen the version which seemed to me to be nearest to the actually sung form.

METRICAL FORMS OF THE ANCIENT SONGS

It should be clear from what has been said above that one cannot accept unconditionally the songs as they are written as being exact reproductions of the way they were sung. In most cases, however, we have nothing to work with except the naked texts—which may very likely be highly abbreviated skeleton versions.

Therefore, it is dangerous to draw any kind of conclusion about the metrical form. However, when we accept the texts uncritically and subject them to metrical analysis, we discover the following facts.

First, the largest number of songs are written in what is known later as the *tanka* form. Around 173 of the 313 songs are in this form. The following (song 183) is an example of a *tanka* (the numbers following each line are the numbers of syllables):

Masurawo no	5
Satsu-ya ta-basami	7
Mukai tachi	5
Iru ya Mato-kata	7
Hama no sayakesa	7
	31

Thus, already in this earliest period of Japanese verse, the *tanka* form is the predominant form numerically.

Next most numerous is what one must call the "irregular *chōka*." A *chōka* is by definition a poem consisting of any number of couplets of 5–7 syllables each, with one 7 syllable line at the end. In this collection, there are only one or two songs which fully meet this definition; all the rest are extremely irregular. I have counted around 68 *chōka*. As an example, I give the text of song 118 (*Kojiki* version):

Kono miki wo	5
Kamikemu hito wa	7
Sono tsuzumi	5
Usu ni tatete	6
Utaitsutsu	5
Kamikere kamo	6
Maitsutsu	4

Kamikere kamo	6
Kono miki no	5
Miki no	3
Aya ni uta-danoshi	8
Sa sa	2

Probably it is correct to say that these irregular *chōka*—differing in meter with each song—are the most authentic and the oldest of the verse forms found in the ancient song literature.

I have discussed on p. 91 the verse form called modernly *Bussoku-seki-ka*; there are 22 songs clearly recorded in this form in this collection. Here is an example (song 132):

Kore no yo wa	5
Utsuri saru to mo	7
Toko towa ni	5
Sa-nokori imase	7
Nochi no yo no tame	7
Mata no yo no tame	7

There are 13 songs in the *kata-uta* verse form, the shortest of all the Japanese verse forms. As an example, I give song 88:

Na ga miko ya	5
Tsubi ni shiramu to	7
Kari wa komurashi	7

Next, there are six songs in the *sedōka* form, which metrically consists of two *Kata-uta*. The example is song 261:

Atarashiki	5
Iname no takumi	7
Kakeshi sumi-nawa	7
Shi ga nakeba	5
Tare ka kakemu yo	7
Atara sumi-nawa	7

Finally, there are around 33 songs which I have had difficulty fitting into any known metrical form.

As a general rule, the translations of the songs have the same number of lines as the originals; therefore the reader can tell for himself what the metrical form is, and I have usually not labeled the form.

Literary Techniques of the Ancient Songs

In general, the primary technical devices used here are not widely divergent from those used in later Japanese poetry.

One aspect which is almost a unique feature, however, is the frequent use of repetition. Many times the same line is repeated twice to heighten the effect.

> With each other as beloved,
> If only we sleep together,
> Then, though like threshed reeds,
> Things go wrong, let them go wrong—
> If only we sleep together.
> (song 49)

Closely allied to this is the frequent use of parallelism.

> Not even untying
>   The cord of my sword,
> Not even untying
>   My cloak,
> I stood there
>   And pushed and shook,
> I stood there
>   And pulled and shoved
> On the wooden door
>   Where the maiden slept.
> (song 4)

Plays on words and puns appear frequently, although the *kake-kotoba* (the so-called "pivot word") technique had not yet come into so great a vogue as later.

The *makura kotoba*, or fixed epithet is already an omnipresent feature of the verse of this period.

It is not surprising that there are many refrains and exclamatory particles.

The musical effect is heightened by the use of alliteration; for example, note the repetition of the vowel *u* in this song (no. 165):

Minato no
Ushio no kudari
Una kudari
Ushiro mo kure ni
Okite ka yukamu

There are even cases of rhyme—perhaps unintentional—as in the following song (no. 18):

Tokoshie ni	a
Kimi mo ae ya mo	b
Isana tori	a
Umi no hama-mo no	b
Yoru toki-doki wo	b

The imagery of the songs is strikingly concrete and close to every-day life, frequently borrowed from hunting, fishing, and agriculture. In no other period of Japanese poetry do we find the white arms of a woman compared with white *daikon* radishes; and sophisticated court poets would hardly think of speaking of irrigation pipes, smelling leeks, snipe-nets, and stinging pepper plants.

In dealing with this imagery, one must avoid regarding it as a mere figure of speech modifying some main idea. The imagery is there more as an intuitive suggestion, as a contrast rather than as an intellectually conceived comparison, and there is often very little grammatical or logical connection between the imagery and the accompanying idea. Y. Okazaki says, in his study of symbolism in ancient Japanese verse, that the natural objects in the ancient songs often seem not to possess any independent significance of their own, but are used as doors leading to a complex state of consciousness lurking in the background. They are used as symbols hinting—very often incoherently—at some intricate, intense mental state.*

ABOUT THE TRANSLATION AND ARRANGEMENT

In translating this material, it was assumed that the reader was primarily interested in a faithful, unembellished translation conveying accurately the overtly expressed meaning (and therefore capable, as is the original, of being interpreted in various different ways), attempting to reproduce to a certain extent the metrical structure, and aiming to recreate, as nearly as possible, the *flavor* of the original.

---

* Yoshie Okazaki, *Nihon shika no shōchō seishin: kodai hen*, Tokyo, 1950, p. 98. See, for example, songs 275 and 276.

With regard to interpetation, modern Japanese authorities were consistently consulted. In no case did I blindly accept the theories of any one authority; theories were carefully and critically examined in order to obtain the most plausible interpretations. In cases where numerous contradictory interpretations exist, I chose the one which seemed to me personally to fit best what I considered to be the spirit of the song itself. Especially valuable were the works of Y. Takeda, T. Aiso, and Y. Tsuchihashi.

The songs from the *Kojiki* and *Nihon Shoki* are usually arranged in Japanese books in the order in which they appear in those documents. There is only one anthology—Takeda's *Zoku-Manyōshū*—in which the entire body of ancient songs, including those outside of the *Kojiki* and *Nihon Shoki*, are arranged in a classification scheme consisting of three sections: "Miscellaneous," "Love Songs," and "Elegies."

In this volume I have, more or less arbitrarily, classified the whole body of songs into nine chapters. I can scarcely claim that this arrangement is better than any other, and there are dozens of cases over which I hesitated. By including a certain song in a certain category, I did not mean to say that it had to belong permanently and irrevocably to this category, but merely intended to group together songs of a broadly similar nature in order to facilitate comparison.

At the beginning of the notes for each song, I have first given the source document or documents. If the song was from either the *Kojiki* or *Nihon Shoki*, I have given its traditional number. Following this, I have given the number assigned to each song in Takeda's *Zoku-Manyōshū*; these numbers are preceded by the letter Z.

In the appendix I have given a finding list for the songs from the *Kojiki* and *Nihon Shoki*. Those using the traditional numbering may use this to locate the translation for each song.

This Wine of Peace,
This Wine of Laughter

Love Songs

Ancient Japanese verse is distinguished for the number and variety of its love songs. Approximately one fifth of the songs in this volume are included here.

Since the songs deal with so many aspects of romantic experience, they defy classification. Nevertheless, besides the large "Miscellaneous" section, I have found enough songs in each category to justify a division under the following four headings: "Songs of Romantic Invitation;" "Songs of Wooing;" "Songs of Reproach;" and "Songs of Longing and Separation."

Songs of Romantic Invitation

Recorded as having been sung at the funeral of the god Ame-no-waka-hiko in order to pacify the anger of the god Aji-shiki-Taka-hikone.

1   By the ford where cross
    The maidens of the country,
    Far away as the heavens—
        Pool on one side of the stony river!—
    In the pool there,
    We spread a net:
    As the eyelets of the net come towards us,
    Come, come towards us!—
        Pool on one side of the stony river!

Recorded as having been sung by Prince Karu when he was captured to be punished for his incestuous relations with Princess Karu.

2   Oh sky-flying
    Karu maidens:
    Oh come and sleep,
    Sleep fully and go,
    Oh maidens of Karu.

A popular song (waza-uta) *sung in the fifth month of the year 670* A.D.
*The song became widespread in the month following a fire which razed Hōryūji Temple; no
doubt the compilers of the* Nihon Shoki *attached some prophetical significance to this* waza-
uta. *However, the song is obviously an independent popular song, perhaps sung to accompany
dancing.*

3   Come out, lass,
    To the celebration
    At the foot of the bridge,
    Mistress Yae-ko
    Of the house of Tamade.

    There will be no regret
    For coming out;
    Come out, lass,
    Mistress Yae-ko
    Of the house of Tamade.

SONGS OF WOOING

Songs 4–8 are a group of closely related songs connected with the mythological accounts of the god Ya-chi-hoko (also called Ō-kuni-nushi and a variety of other names) and his romantic adventures. The first three deal with the god's wooing of Princess Nunakawa.

After the god had already gained Suseri-hime, the daughter of the god Susa-no-wo, as his chief wife, he again set out to woo Princess Nunakawa of the land of Koshi. Song 4 is the song which he sang upon arrival at her house.

4 The god
    Ya-chi-hoko,
  Unable to find a wife
    In the land of the eight islands,
  Hearing that
    In the far-away
  Land of Koshi
    There was a wise maiden,
  Hearing that
    There was a fair maiden,
  Set out
    To woo her,
  Went out
    To win her.

  Not even untying
    The cord of my sword,
  Not even untying
    My cloak,
  I stood there
    And pushed and shook,
  I stood there
    And pulled and shoved
  On the wooden door
    Where the maiden slept.

  Then, on the verdant mountains

The *nuye* bird sang.
The bird of the field,
    The pheasant resounded.
The bird of the yard,
    The cock crowed.

Ah, how hateful
    These birds for crying!
Would that I could make them
    Stop their accursed singing!

These are
The words,
The words handed down
By the *ishitafu ya*
Ama messenger clan.

Songs 5 and 6 are both replies of Princess Nunakawa to the preceding song. Some authorities have even regarded them as being one single song.

5   Oh god
            Ya-chi-hoko!
        Since I am but a woman,
            Supple like the pliant grass,
        My heart is all a-flutter
            Like the birds of the seashore.
        Although now I may be
            A free, selfish bird of my own,
        Later, I shall be yours,
            A bird ready to submit to your will.
        Therefore, my lord, be patient;
            Do not die of love.

        These are
        The words,
        The words handed down
        By the *ishitafu ya*
        Ama messenger clan.

6 As soon as the sun
  Hides behind the verdant mountains,
Then jet-black
  Night will come.
Smiling resplendently
  Like the morning sun,
With your arms
  White as a rope of *taku* fibers,
  You will embrace
My breast, thrilling with youth,
  Soft as the light snow;
We shall embrace and entwine our bodies.
Your jewel-like hands
  Will twine with mine,
And, your legs outstretched,
  You will lie and sleep.
Therefore, my lord,
  Do not yearn.
Oh god
  Ya-chi-hoko!

These are
The words,
The words handed down.

The chief wife of the god, Princess Suseri, was intensely jealous. The god, stung by her taunts, started out to go up from Izumo to the land of Yamato. When he had completed his attire, he placed one foot on the saddle of his horse and one foot in the stirrup and sang this song.

7 All dressed up
   In my jet-black clothes,
  When I look down at my breast,
   Like a bird of the sea,
  Flapping its wings,
   This garment will not do;
  I throw it off
   By the billowy beach.

  All dressed up
   In my blue clothes,
  Blue like the *soni* bird,
   When I look down at my breast,
  Like a bird of the sea,
   Flapping its wings,
  This also will not do;
  I throw it off
   By the billowy beach.

  All dressed up
   In my clothes dyed
  With the juice
   Of pounded *atane* plants
   Grown in the mountain fields,
  Now when I look down at my breast,
   Like a bird of the sea,
  Flapping its wings,
   This will do.

  Beloved wife of mine,
  When I go off

With my retainers
Flocking like flocking birds,

When I go off
With my retainers
Accompanied like birds of a company,
Although you may say
That you will not cry—
Your head drooping,
Like the lone reed of *susuki* grass
On the mountain side,
You will cry,
And your crying will rise
Just as the morning rain
Rises into a mist.
Oh my young wife
Like the young grass.

These are
The words,
The words handed down.

The conciliatory reply of Princess Suseri, who thereby was able to dissuade her spouse from leaving.

The Kojiki *narrative before the song says that Princess Suseri, having heard song 7, approached with a large wine-cup, which she offered while singing this song. After the song, the couple pledged their troth with wine-cups and embraced each other around the neck, remaining enshrined thus until the present day. (Evidently refers to those representations of deities hugging each other which are mentioned by Tachibana Moribe in his* Itsu-no-Koto-waki.*)*

8   Oh god
     Ya-chi-hoko!
     Oh my Ō-kuni-nushi!
   Since you
     Are a man,
   On all the islands
     You row around,
   On each and every promontory
     You go around,
   You must have wives
     Like young grass.

   But I,
     Being a woman,
   Have no man
     Besides you,
   Have no husband
     Besides you.

   Under silken curtains,
     The fluffy ones,
   Under covers of *mushi* fibers,
     The soft ones,
   Under covers of *taku* fibers,
     The rustling ones,
   My breast, thrilling with youth,
     Soft as the light snow,

You will embrace
  With your arms
  White as a rope of *taku* fibers.
We shall embrace and entwine our bodies.
Your jewel-like hands
  Will twine with mine.
With your legs outstretched,
  Oh come, my lord, and sleep!

Partake, oh my lord,
  Of the abundant wine!

The Imperial Prince Magari-no-Ohine (later Emperor Ankan) in 513 A.D. wedded the Imperial Princess Kasuga. On a moonlight night they held converse, unaware when the dawn came. Elegant style suddenly appeared in the prince's words and he broke into song.

9   Unable to find a wife
              In the land of the eight islands,
          Hearing that
              In the land of Kasuga
          Of the spring sunshine,
              There was a fair maiden,
          Hearing that
              There was a good maiden:

          The doors of wood
              Of flourishing *hi* trees—
          Pushing them open,
              I entered
          And embraced her legs,
              Taking her as wife,
          And embraced her head,
              Taking her as wife,
          Letting my beloved's hands
              Embrace me,
          And embracing my beloved
              With my hands,
          Like clinging vines,
              Mingling and entwining—

          Just then,
              When I was sleeping well,
          The bird of the yard,
              The cock crowed,
          The bird of the field,
              The pheasant resounded.

          Already, before even telling
          Of my love,
          The day has dawned, my beloved.

SONGS OF REPROACH

The god Ninigi doubted the faithfulness of his spouse, Ko-no-hana-saku-ya-hime, who had become pregnant in one night. The spouse proved her innocence by ordeal, but thereafter refused to consort with the god. The god thereupon sang this song of reproach.

10   The sea-weeds of the offing
    Come seeking the shore;
    But you provide
    No sleeping place,
    You plover of the beach!

Attributed in both Kojiki *and* Nihon Shoki *to Emperor Nintoku, who sang it in reproach to his consort Iwa-no-hime after she had fled to Yamashiro in a fit of jealousy.*

11   The maiden of Yamashiro
     Of many mountain peaks
    With a wooden-handled hoe
     Digs up *daikon* radishes:
    White like these radishes
     Are your white arms—
    If I had not embraced these arms,
     Then you might say you know me not.

SONGS OF LONGING AND SEPARATION

12–14 are songs connected with an old Japanese sea-wife legend. Ho-wori-no-mikoto returned from the place of the Sea-god, whose daughter he had married. Later, the sea-wife princess Toyo-tama emerged from the sea to give birth to her child on land. She warned her husband not to set eyes on her, but he broke the taboo and gazed upon her as she was giving birth, finding her transformed into a huge crocodile. Filled with bitterness, the princess returned to the sea, later sending this song of yearning.

12   Beautiful are bright jewels;
      Even their cord seems to sparkle.
      But I prefer pearls,
      For the awesome beauty
      Of your pearl-like form.

13   Although they say
      That you have the radiance
      Of bright jewels,
      The beauty of your form
      Is even more awesome.

The song sung by Ho-wori-no-mikoto in longing for his sea-wife who had returned to her watery homeland.

14   As long as I have life,
      I shall never forget
      My beloved, with whom I slept
      On an island where wild ducks,
      Birds of the offing, came to land.

This and the following song are attributed to the hero Yamato Takeru, who sang them (traditionally in the year 113 A.D.) while in the palace of Sakawori in Kai, in yearning for his spouse Miyazu-hime, who was then in Narumi.

15 The elder maiden of Higami
    By the bay of Ayuchi—
    Expecting me to come,
    She must be waiting up—
    Alas, poor elder maiden!

16 When I look towards Narumi Bay,
    It is far away.
    Rowing earnestly,
    In this evening tide
    Can I cross over?

In 291 A.D., E-hime, the beloved concubine of Emperor Ōjin, was granted leave to return to visit her parents in the land of Kibi. The Emperor made this song upon her departure, while standing on a high tower and watching her boat depart from Naniwa (modern Ōsaka).

17   The island of Awaji
            Lies next to its mate;
        The island of Azuki
            Lies next to its mate.
        Ah, what good islands!
        But who
            Has caused our separation?—
        When I was meeting fondly
            With my beloved, the maiden of Kibi!

A song sung in the year 422 A.D. by lady So-tōri, a favorite of Emperor Ingyō, when the Emperor's visits began to diminish in number because of the jealousy of the Empress.

18   Shall we always
        Be able to meet, my lord?
        Ah no—as the sea-weeds
        Of the ocean approach the shore—
        Only from time to time.

*After the death of Emperor Ingyo in 453 A.D. Prince Ki-nashi-no-Karu,
the heir to the throne, was discovered to have had incestuous relations with his sister, Princess
Karu. The prince (or, in some accounts, the princess) was banished to Iyo (a part of present
Shikoku). This song was sung by the prince as he was about to be banished; or, according to
the* Nihon Shoki, *by the prince when the princess was banished.*

19   If the great lord
            Is exiled to an island,
        (The excess ships)
            I will return.
        Leave my sitting-mat alone!

        Although outwardly I speak
        Of sitting-mats, I really mean:
        Leave my wife alone!

Attributed in the Kojiki *to Princess Karu, who, after Prince Karu had
been banished, set out to go after him, singing this song.*

20   Since you have set out,
        Many days have passed.
        Like the *yama-tazu* tree,
        I will go in search of you:
        I am unable to wait.

When Princess Karu had caught up with Prince Karu, Prince Karu sang this song of yearning.

21   On Mount Hatsuse
            Of the hidden country,
        On the large ridges
            Are erected banners,
        On the small ridges
            Are erected banners.

        Alas, my beloved spouse,
            Relying on our troth
        As upon an immobile mountain ridge!

        Like a *tsuki* bow
            Reclining,
        Like an *azusa* bow
            Standing up

        Later I shall take you close,
        Alas, my beloved spouse!

Also sung by Prince Karu when re-united with Princess Karu in exile. After singing this song, they both committed suicide.

22   On the river of Hatsuse
         Of the hidden country,
   In the upper shallows
         A sacred post was staked,
   In the lower shallows
         A true post was staked.

   On the sacred post
         Was hung a mirror,
   On the true post
         Was hung a jewel.

   My beloved,
         Who is to me as a mirror,
   My spouse,
         Who is to me as a jewel—

   Only if I hear
         That she is there,
   Do I wish to go home,
         Do I yearn for my country.

Songs 23–26 are recorded in a fragment of the Tango Fudoki *quoted in the* Shoku Nihongi; *all four are connected with the legend of the boy of Urashima (known today as Urashima Tarō), a Japanese Rip Van Winkle.*

The boy of Urashima, of Mizu-no-e in the land of Tango, one day went out fishing. He caught a beautifully colored tortoise, which changed while he slept into a lovely princess. The princess took him to dwell with her in an island in the sea, and after three years he returned to his home, only to find that 300 years had elapsed. Breaking the taboo, he opened the magic box which the princess had given him on parting; immediately a shape like an orchid issued from the box and went flying away in a cloud. The boy wept, realizing that he had forever forfeited his chance of being re-united with the princess in the Eternal World.

23   Towards the Eternal World
The clouds shift across—
Bearing across the words
Uttered by the boy of Urashima
Of Mizu-no-e.

24   Up towards Yamato
Blows the wind,
Scattering the clouds;
Though apart like these clouds,
Oh, do not forget me!

25   Yearning for the maiden,
As I open the door in the morning,
And stand there still,
I can hear the sound of the waves
On the beach of the Eternal World.

26   If the boy of Urashima
Of Mizu-no-e
Had only not opened
The jeweled box,
He might have met her again.

During the reign of Emperor Kimmei (539–571 A.D.), a man of the land of Mino married a woman who eventually revealed her true nature as a fox disguised in human form. After being found out, the fox ran off, still dragging her pink petticoat behind her. The husband, watching the fox running away, sang this song.

27   Yearning has all
            Fallen upon me:
            Because of the maiden,
            Visible far in the distance,
            Who has left me.

Attributed to Oto-tachibana-hime, the wife of Yamato Takeru. As the couple were crossing the sea between the Miura and Bōsō peninsulas, a fierce storm arose, preventing the ship from going on. Oto-tachibana-hime gave her life as a sacrifice to the Sea-god, whereupon the boat was immediately able to proceed. This is the song she sang on parting from her husband.

28   Oh, you, my lord, alas—
            You who once, standing among the flames
            Of the burning fire, spoke my name
            On the mountain-surrounded
            Plain of Sagamu!

Kuro-hime, a favorite of Emperor Nintoku (reigned traditionally 313–399 A.D.), fearing the jealousy of the Empress, Iwa-no-hime, fled to her homeland in Kibi. The Emperor ascended a high tower and watched her depart, singing this song.

29
In the offing,
The small boats are stretched in a row;
In one of them,
Masazuko my beloved
Descends to her native land.

The Emperor followed after Kuro-hime to her native place in Kibi (see songs 277 and 40). When he was about to depart, Kuro-hime sang this song.

30
Up towards Yamato
Blows the west wind,
Scattering the clouds;
Though parted like these clouds,
Shall I ever forget you?

Again Kuro-hime sang in parting from the Emperor (follows the preceding song).

31
Whose spouse is this
Who goes towards Yamato?
Whose spouse is this
Who goes, like an underground stream,
Stealthily, silently?

Sung by Prince Karu as he was about to be banished to Iyo.

32   The sky-flying
Birds are also messengers:
When you hear
The cry of the crane,
Call my name to it.

In the Kojiki *account this song follows directly after song 19 and is attributed to Princess So-tōshi (Princess Karu).*

33   Oh, do not go, for you may tread
On the oyster shells
On the beach of Ahine
Of the summer grass—
Spend the night and return in the morning!

MISCELLANEOUS LOVE SONGS

The Emperor Jimmu sojourned one night at the house of Princess Isuke-
yori by the Sai river. When, later on, the Princess entered the Palace, the Emperor sang this
song recalling their first union.

34   In a humble little house
     Nestling in a reed-plain,
     Spreading out the clean
     Rustling sedge-mats,
     The two of us slept.

Emperor Ōjin, on his visit to Afumi (Ōmi), came to the village of Kohata,
where he met a beautiful maiden upon the road. He asked her name and promised to visit her
house on his return the following day. The next day, the maiden's father feasted the Emperor,
and the maiden presented wine to the Emperor, who thereupon sang this song as he accepted the
wine. Afterwards, the Emperor and the maiden were united. Her name was Ya-gaha-e-hime,
and she bore the prince Uji-no-waki-iratsuko.

35   This crab—
          Where is he from?
     He is a crab
          From far-away Tsunuga.
     Moving along sideways,
          Where is he going?

     Arriving at Ichiji island,
          Arriving at Mishima island,
     Like the *miho* birds,
          Diving into the water, panting,
     As I went ahead
          With rapid strides
     Along the Sasanami road—
     On the Kohata road
          I met a maiden.

Viewed from the back,
    Her form was straight like a shield;
Her teeth were white
    Like *shii* acorns, like water-chestnuts.
Her eye-brows were painted,
    Painted down thickly
With clay from the Wani district
    Near Ichi-i—
Not with the top-clay,
    Which was too reddish,
Nor with the lower layers of clay,
    Which was too black,
But with the clay
    From the very middle layers,
Which was prepared
    Without exposing it to a strong fire.
This was the young woman I met!

And the girl whom I saw
    And wished this about,
The girl whom I saw
    And wished that about—
Is now, much to my delight,
    Here opposite me,
    Is here close by my side!

*The Emperor Ōjin in 282 A.D. summoned from the land of Hyūga a beau-
tiful maiden called Kami-naga-hime. The Imperial Prince Ō-sazaki (later Emperor Nintoku)
saw the maiden and was struck by her beauty. The Emperor gave a feast and, singing this song,
presented the maiden to the Prince.*

36   Come, my lads,
      To pick wild *hiru* plants.
    To pick *hiru* plants,
      As we go along the road,
    There is a fragrant
      Flowering *tachibana* tree.

    Its upper branches
      Are withered by the birds nesting;
    Its lower branches
      Are withered by people plucking them.

    But the three-chestnut
      Middle branches—
    Like these best branches
      Is the ruddy maiden—
    Ah come
      And take her!

The Kojiki *attributes this song to Emperor Ōjin, who sang it immediately
after the preceding song.*

37   Not knowing that the one
      Who stakes out dam-posts
    Had set out a post in the pond of Yosami
      Of the accumulated waters;
    Not knowing that the roots
      Of the *nunaha* had grown thus far—
    Ah my heart—
      How foolish it has been;
      Now I am filled with regret!

After Prince Ō-sazaki had gained the maiden Kami-naga-hime, he sang this and the following song.

38   The maiden of Kohada
                Of the far-away country,
                Whose fame rumbled afar
                Like the thunder—
                Now lies by my side.

39   I think lovingly
                Of the maiden of Kohada
                Of the far-away country,
                Who slept by my side
                Without resisting.

Emperor Nintoku went along the Inland Sea to the land of Kibi (present Okayama prefecture), where Kuro-hime entertained him (see songs 29–30, 277). When Kuro-hime went out to the mountains to pick greens for a soup to present the Emperor, he followed her out and sang this song.

40   What a delight
To pick together
With the girl of Kibi
The greens growing
On the mountain fields.

Emperor Nintoku sent this song by messenger to his consort Iwa-no-hime, who had fled in a fit of jealousy.

41   On the high place
    Of Mimoro,
The Plain of the Great Boar—
    In the belly
Of the great boar,
    Next to the liver, the heart—
In our hearts, at least,
Can we help but think of each other?

Sung by Emperor Nintoku in sympathy with Princess Yata.

Princess Yata became Empress in 350 A.D. after the death of the former Empress, Iwa-no-hime, in 347 A.D. But Princess Yata remained childless, and this song is thought to refer to this.

42   The lone sedge
Of Yata
Has no offspring;
Will it wither as it stands?
Alas, poor sedge-grove!

Although outwardly I speak
Of sedge-groves, I really mean:
Alas, pure maiden!

The reply to the preceding song by Princess Yata.

43   The lone sedge
Of Yata cares not
Though she be alone.

If only her lord
Think it good, she cares not
Though she be alone.

The princess So-tōshi, a favorite of Emperor Ingyō, was dwelling in a separate palace at Fujiwara to avoid the rage of the jealous Empress. In the second month of 419 A.D., the Emperor went to Fujiwara to visit her. That night, the princess was alone thinking of the Emperor; unaware of his presence, she sang this song.

The activities of spiders were regarded as omens as to whether a lover would come or not.

44   My beloved
    Must be coming this evening.
    For the behavior
    Of the spiders on the bamboo-grass
    Is striking this evening.

The Emperor, hearing the above song, his heart filled with love, sang this.

45   Untying
    My finely embroidered
    Brocade cord,
    I slept, not many times,
    But one night only.

The next morning, the Emperor saw the cherry blossoms by the spring and sang this song.

46   Loving as I do
    The beautifully flowering cherry tree;
    Loving you as I do,
    I regret that I did not love you earlier,
    You maiden whom I love.

The Kojiki *and* Nihon Shoki *both attribute the song to Prince Ki-nashi-no-Karu (see song 19), who used it to declare his passion for his sister Princess Karu.*

47   Making a mountain paddy,
              Because the mountain is high,
              An irrigation pipe is run
              Underneath the ground, secretly—

                  Secretly I have visited
                    My beloved;
                  Secretly I have wept
                    For my spouse.

              Tonight at last
                  I fondle her body with ease.

Attributed to Prince Karu (see song 19).

48   The hail beating down
              On the bamboo grass
              Sounding *tasi-dasi*—
              After sleeping with her to the full,
              Then, even if she leaves me . . .

Following song 48; attributed to Prince Karu.

49   With each other as beloved,
              If only we sleep together,
              Then, though like threshed reeds,
              Things go wrong, let them go wrong—
              If only we sleep together.

Attributed to Prince Karu after he was taken prisoner; or in the Nihon
Shoki, *when his affair with Princess Karu was discovered and she was banished to Iyo.*

50   Oh sky-flying
    Karu maiden—
    Should I cry loudly,
    People would know.
    Like the pigeons
    On Hasa mountain,
    I cry secretly.

*As Emperor Yūryaku was going to visit the Princess Waka-Kusaka-be
(who became Empress in 457 A.D.) at her home in Kusaka, the Princess sent word that it was
inauspicious for the Emperor to progress with his back to the sun, and promised that she would
set out immediately to go and serve him. Then, as he was about to return to his palace, he
stood atop the mountain incline and sang this song, which he sent by messenger to the Princess.*

51   In the valleys
      Here and there
    Between the mountains this side
      Of Kusakabe
    And the rush-matting
      Heguri mountain—
    There stands a thriving
      Wide-leaved oak tree.
    At its foot
      Grows entwined bamboo;
    At its sides
      Grows luxuriant bamboo.
    Entwined bamboo:
      We did not sleep entwined;
    Luxuriant bamboo:
      We did not sleep luxuriantly.
    But later we will sleep twined—
    Ah that beloved spouse of mine!

Once when Emperor Yūryaku went to the River Miwa (now the Hase River in Nara prefecture), he met a beautiful woman washing clothes. When he asked her name, she said it was Hiketa-no-Aka-iko. The Emperor commanded her to wait for his summons and not to take another husband. The maiden waited for eighty years in vain; finally, realizing that there was no longer any hope, she went to the Emperor to declare her faithfulness. The Emperor, pitying her, wished to favor her, but was unable to because of her great age, and instead bestowed a song upon her.

52   The field of Hiketa
     Where young chestnut trees grow:
     When I was young
     Would that I had slept with her—
     But now I am old.

When Emperor Yūryaku went to Kasuga to woo Odo-hime, daughter of the ruler of the Wani clan, the maiden ran away and hid on a hill. The Emperor made this song. That is why that hill is called Kana-suki-no-Oka, or Metal Plough Hill.

53   The maiden
     Is hiding on the hill—
     Oh for five hundred
     Metal ploughs:
     I would plough it up!

Attributed to Prince Waka-sazaki (Emperor Muretsu), who sang it in praise of Kage-hime. Kage-hime had already formed an illicit union with a youth called Shibi.

54   Kage-hime, seated
       By the *koto*—
       If she were a jewel,
       She would be the jewel of my desires,
       The white pearl of the abalone.

Song of rejection by Shibi on behalf of the maiden Kage-hime.

55   The sash of *shitsu* cloth
       Of the great lord
       Is tied and hangs:
       There is not anyone
       Who thinks of him.

Reply of Princess Kasuga to song 9.
I have included it here because of the close resemblance of its final portion
to song 55.

56   Down the river Hatsuse
        Of the hidden country
Came floating a bamboo tree,
      A flourishing bamboo, a many-sectioned bamboo.
Its lower part
      Was made into a *koto;*
Its upper part
      Was made into a flute—
Playing the flute,
      When I climbed
To the top of Mt. Mimoro
      And looked out—
In the pond
      Of Ihare,
The fish
      In the water
Came up and sighed.

Our great lord
      The Emperor
Wears around his waist
      A finely embroidered sash,
Which is tied and hangs—
      Anyone at all
      Would come up and sigh!

*After Ōtomo-no-Sadehiko had been sent (in 537 A.D., according to the
Nihon Shoki) to do battle in Korea, his wife Oto-hime was visited every night by a man
closely resembling him; after sleeping with her, he would go back in the morning. Oto-hime,
suspicious of this nocturnal visitor, tied a thread to the hem of his garment and followed its
path. Finally the thread led her to the pond on top of Hire-furu Peak. Inside the pond was
sleeping a dragon with the body of a human and the head of a dragon. Immediately the dragon
turned into a human and sang this song. Later, when a searching party came looking for Oto-
hime, neither the dragon nor the girl was anywhere to be seen, but there was a human corpse
at the bottom of the pond, which everyone said was that of Oto-hime.*

57   The girl Oto-hime
            Of Shinohara:
            After we have slept together
            For one night—
            Then I will let her return home.

*In 644 A.D., the district of Upper Shiki in Yamato reported that, several
years before, a man came upon a monkey taking a nap on Mt. Miwa. He took the monkey
by the elbow, but did it no bodily harm. The monkey, its eyes closed, sang this song. The man,
amazed, set it free and came away. The song was a portent, predicting that many years later
the sons of Prince Shōtoku would be surrounded on Mt. Ikoma by Soga-no-Iruka (in 643 A.D.).*

58   Would that the lad
            Standing on yonder ridge
            Would take my hand
            In his soft hands.

            Whose rough hands,
            Rough hands are these,
            Which are taking my hand?

In the sixth month of 644 A.D., the priestesses and priests of the whole country gathered as Soga-no-Emishi, the prime minister of the time, was about to cross a bridge and contended with each other in addressing to him mysterious utterances, all speaking at once so that their words could not be heard clearly. This was interpreted as an omen of a change. At that time there were three waza-uta.

59   I slept with someone
                Without disturbing
                The pheasants
                In the sparse plain yonder;
                But others have caused a flurry.

The third of the waza-uta.

60   I do not know the face
                Nor the house
                Of the man
                Who led me into the woods
                And did it.

During 653 A.D., the Prince Imperial (later Emperor Tenchi) petitioned Emperor Kōtoku to move the capital from Naniwa to Yamato, but the Emperor refused. Thereupon the Prince Imperial on his own accord moved to Yamato, taking with him the Empress Dowager (Empress Kōgyoku) and the Empress Hashibito, wife of Emperor Kōtoku. The ministers and officials all followed them. The Emperor, resenting this, sent this song to his wife, Empress Hashibito.

61   The pony which I kept,
                Harnessed with a wooden collar—
                I never led her out:
                The pony which I kept—
                Has someone seen her?

One of the waza-uta *which were sung at the time of the death of Emperor Tenchi (late in 671 A.D.).*

62   A vine thicket
                Through which the brown pony
                Hesitates to go:
                Why send messages?
                Better to do it directly.

The Hitachi Fudoki *gives this song in connection with a stone cave inside a forest on Mount Asiho in Hitachi.*

63   If prudish tongues are irksome,
        We shall go together
        And hide in the cave
        On Mount Wo-hatsuse:
        Do not yearn, my beloved.

The Hitachi Fudoki *gives songs 64 and 65 as songs sung when the young men and women climb Mount Tsukuba in spring and autumn and disport themselves.*

64   The girl who promised
        To meet me
        On Mount Tsukuba—
        Was it because she listened to someone else?—
        Did not meet and sleep with me.

65   This night
        When I must sleep
        On Mount Tsukuba
        Without a partner—
        Would that it would soon dawn!

Songs 66 and 67 are given in the Hitachi Fudoki *as songs sung by the local inhabitants when they come in great numbers to disport themselves on the lovely beach of Takahama in Hitachi.*

66   The waves come near
    The beach of Takahama,
    The waves of the offing:
    Though they come near, I will not go near—
    Since my heart has gone near the maiden!

67   The low winds rustle
    On the beach of Takahama:
    I long for a lover,
    Someone to call my spouse—
    But she has called me ugly!

Songs 68 and 69 are recorded in the Hitachi Fudoki *as part of the legend of a pine grove called Wotome no Matsu-bara, or Maiden's Pine Grove. Long ago there was a young man and a young woman—the girl's name was Unakami-no-Aze-no-wotome. They were both famed for their beauty of form, and had long heard of each other and were filled with longing for each other. After much time had elapsed, they finally met at an* utagaki *(see note to no. 64) celebration. At this time, the boy sang this song.*

68   The maiden Azeko
     Is seen hanging sacred *yū* cloth
     On the pine trees of Aze
     And waving it towards me,
     As she dances . . .

    This is the reply sung by the maiden.
    After exchanging these songs, the couple hid under the pine trees and gave vent to their pent-up feelings. When dawn came, ashamed of being discovered, they were transformed into pine trees.

69   Even though you stand
     Amid the tide,
     My beloved brother,
     Hidden among the myriad isles,
     You will know me when you see me.

Ceremonial and Religious Songs

In this section I have included all songs which seemed to be primarily intended for some ceremonial or religious purposes.

First, under "Ceremonial Songs," I have given songs which seemed to me to be meant to accompany the motions of official or religious ceremonies.

Under "Songs of Blessing," I included those laudatory or congratulatory songs which were intended to bring down divine blessings.

Then, under the headings "Songs Praising Persons or Gods," "Songs Praising Lands or Countries," and "Songs Praising Palaces," I grouped together songs which were sung in order to praise and thus to bring about blessings.

Finally, I have a section "Wine-praising and Drinking Songs," where I included all songs connected with wine and drinking, which played an important role in religious and official ceremonies.

When Ama-terasu-ō-mikami, the Sun Goddess, retired into the Heavenly Cave, plunging the universe into darkness, the gods sang and danced before the cave. When the Sun Goddess, curious at the commotion, peered outside, she was pulled forcibly out of her hiding place, and the universe again became bright. Hereupon the gods rejoiced, singing this song.

70   Ah, how pleasant!
               How delightful!
               How pure!
               Oke!

In the year 90 B.C., worship was paid the god Ō-mono-nushi (same as Ya-chi-hoko and Ō-kuni-nushi) at Mount Miwa, in the presence of Emperor Sūjin. Afterwards a feast was held in the shrine of the god. Following the feast, the various high officials sang this song.

71   The shrine of Miwa
               Of the tasty wine—
               Would that I could go out
               Of its shrine doors in the morning—
               The shrine doors of Miwa.

After the preceding song, Emperor Sūjin sang this song. After that, they opened the doors of the shrine, and the Emperor departed.

72   The shrine of Miwa
               Of the tasty wine—
               After morning has come,
               Push them open—
               The shrine doors of Miwa.

The account of the Kogo Shūi *attributes version A to the reign of Emperor Sūjin (traditionally 97–30 B.C.). The courtiers sang this song at an all-night feast in honor of the removal of the goddess Ama-terasu-ō-mikami to the village of Kasanui in Yamato.*

The Kogo Shūi *gives version B as a corrupt version sung at the present time (that is, around 807 A.D.).*

73a   The priests
               All through this long night,
               All night long,
               How excellent the sacred wine they drink,
               All through this long night.

73b   The great formal robes
               Of the priests,
               Hanging below their knees—
               How excellent as they walk,
               The great formal robes.

Songs 74 and 75 are recorded in a work compiled in 804 A.D. which chronicles the ceremonies of the Inner Shrine at Ise. The two songs were performed in connection with a banquet held every year after the festival of the 17th day of the 6th month.

74   In the shrine of Isuzu
Of the bell-bracelet,
As the food-offerings are presented,
The gourds are struck,
Reverberating through the shrine.

75   The sound
Of the gourds
Struck for the pleasure
Of the courtiers
Reverberates through the shrine.

Recorded in the Kinkafu *with the musical name* Ise no kamu-uta *(or:* kami-uta*), literally "divine song of Ise."*

The meaning of the song is almost completely unintelligible. There is little doubt that it was a religious song used in the ceremonies of the Ise shrine.

76   *Sabakaru ya*
            The goddess Ōhirume's
            Fore-runner
            Fore-runner
            Yo yo yo yo
            Yo yo yo yo
            Fore runner
            Fore runner
            Fore-runner
            Fore-runner
            Living willow-tree
            Living willow-tree
            Living willow-tree
            Fore-runner

The first of the two songs given by the Emperor to the old woman Hiketa-no-Aka-iko (see song 52).

77   Under the oaks,
              Under the sacred oaks
              Of Mimoro:
              How awesome—
              The oak-forest maidens!

Recorded in the Kojiki *as the reply which Aka-iko, weeping bitterly, offered to the Emperor. The* Kinkafu, *after giving the* Kojiki *account, offers as a more probable account that it was sung by Emperor Suinin (reigned traditionally 29 B.C.–70 A.D.) when he worshipped at Mount Miwa.*

78   At Mimoro
              Is built a jeweled fence—
              Some is left over:
              On whom will you rely,
              You servants of the deity?

When Emperor Yūryaku (reigned traditionally 456–479 A.D.) visited the Palace of Yoshino (in 460?), he met on the bank of the Yoshino river a beautiful maiden, whom he summoned and took into his service. The next time he visited Yoshino, he purposely stopped at the spot where he had met the maiden, erected a dais, and sat down and played the koto *himself while the maiden danced. Because the maiden danced well, the Emperor made this song.*

79   Seated on the dais,
            With divine hands
            Is played the *koto*,
            To which dances the maiden:
            Would that this would last eternally!

When Emperor Temmu (reigned 673–686 A.D.) was in the palace of Yoshino, he played the koto *at eventide and was carried away with enjoyment. While he was playing, a cloud arose on the mountains, and a vision appeared—visible to the Emperor alone—of what appeared to be a Chinese fairy dancing to the music. Because the dancer raised her sleeves five times, the dance was called* Go-sechi *("five times"?). This was the song accompanying the dance.*

80   The maidens
            Act maiden-like.
            Winding jewels of Kara
            Around their wrists,
            They act maiden-like.

According to the historical work Shoku Nihongi, *this song was sung to* koto *accompaniment by those below the sixth rank at a banquet given on the 16th day of the New Year of the year 742 A.D. by Emperor Shōmu.*

81   At the beginning
Of the new year—
In this manner,
Let us reverently serve,
Until ten thousand ages pass!

According to the account in the introduction to the Kokinshū, *this song was sung by Wani, the Korean scholar, in amazement when Emperor Nintoku and his brother both declined to assume the throne in deference to each other for three years (this was in 313 A.D.).*

82   By the bay of Naniwa
They are blooming—these flowers.
Winter seclusion over,
Now that spring has come,
They are blooming—these flowers.

SONGS OF BLESSING

A song expressing loyalty to the Emperor handed on by the Ōtomo and Saheki clans. The song is quoted with approval in an Imperial edict by Emperor Shōmu in the year 749 as an example of the traditional loyalty inspiring these two clans.

83   If we go by sea,
              We shall become corpses in the brine.
          If we go over the mountains,
              We shall become corpses over which grass grows.
          But we shall die
              For the sake of our lord.
              And we will not die a peaceful death.

Quoted in the Hitachi Fudoki *as a song of blessing sung by Mi-oya-no-kami, the ancestral god, about Mount Tsukuba. The following legend precedes the song. When Mi-oya-no-kami was visiting the various gods he was refused lodging by the god of Mount Fuji, who gave as an excuse that his house was observing a taboo* (mono-imi) *in preparation for the harvest festival. Mi-oya-no-kami pronounced a curse on Mount Fuji and went on to Mount Tsukuba, the god of which, despite the taboo, entertained him warmly. Hereupon, Mi-oya-no-kami, overjoyed, sang this song. That is why to this day no one climbs the continually snow-capped Mount Fuji, but the people all come to Mount Tsukuba to sing and dance, to eat and drink.*

84   How dear my descendants!
              How lofty the divine palace!
          Even with heaven and earth,
              Together with the sun and moon.
          The people assemble in joy;
              Food and drink is abundant.
          For all generations without end,
              Day by day ever more flourishing,
          Until myriads of years hence
              The joy will not cease.

Emperor Yūryaku (reigned traditionally 456–479 A.D.) was holding a feast underneath a luxuriant tsuki *tree at Hatsuse. An* uneme *(court lady presented to the court by each local clan) of Mie in the land of Ise presented the Emperor's wine-cup. Unknown to her, a leaf of the* tsuki *tree fell into the wine-cup which she gave to the Emperor. The Emperor was enraged and about to kill the* uneme, *when she said: "Do not kill me; I have something to say." Thereupon she sang this song, and because of it her crime was forgiven her.*

85   The Palace of Hishiro
            At Makimuku
Is a palace where shines
    The morning sun,
Is a palace where is brilliant
    The evening sun,
Is a palace where the roots
    Of the bamboo are plentiful and abundant,
Is a palace where the roots
    Of the trees are long and extended,
Is a palace built
    Pounding much foundation soil.

By the palace of wood
    Of flourishing *hi* trees,
The Hall of the New Grain,
    There is growing
A luxuriant
    Tsuki tree:
Its upper branches
    Spread out covering the heavens;
Its middle branches
    Spread out covering the Eastern lands;
Its lower branches
    Spread out covering the country regions.

The leaves at the tip
    Of the upper branches
Touch down
    On the middle branches;

The leaves at the tip
    Of the middle branches
Touch down
    On the lower branches;
The leaves at the tip
    Of the lower branches
Drop, as floating oil
    Into the beautiful jeweled cup
Presented
    By the girl of Mie
    Of the silken garments—
And falling into the liquid,
    The waters churning,
    Churning around:
This, too—
    How awesome,
On high-shining
    Prince of the Sun.

These are
The words,
The words handed down.

When a wild goose laid an egg in the year 362 A.D., Emperor Nintoku summoned Takeshi-Uchi-no-sukune and addressed this song of inquiry to him.

86   Oh lord of Uchi
               Of the jewel cutting—
You are the most venerable
               Of this age;
You are the oldest
               In the land.
Have you heard
               Of a wild goose laying an egg
In the Dragon-fly Island,
               The land of Yamato?

The song with which Takeshi-Uchi-no-sukune replied to the Emperor's song of inquiry.

87   Oh high shining
               Child of the Sun—
True it is
               That you inquire of me;
Right it is
               That you inquire of me;
I am the most venerable
               Of this age.
I have never heard
               Of a wild goose laying an egg
In the sky-full
               Land of Yamato.

Song sung by Takeshi-Uchi-no-sukune while playing a koto *given him by the Emperor.*

88
That my lord
Should rule with long life
The wild goose seemingly laid the egg.

Princes Oke (Emperor Ninken) and Woke (Emperor Kensō), the grandsons of Emperor Richū, fled and went into hiding because their father, Ichi-no-be-no-Oshi-ha-no-miko, was killed by Emperor Yūryaku. The two princes fled to the land of Harima, concealed their names and rank, and were employed incognito *as servants of a local ruler, Shijimi-no-Miyake-no-obito. In 481 A.D., the second year of the reign of Emperor Seimei, their employer held a dedication celebration for a new house in the presence of the governor of the land of Harima, Iyo-no-kume-be-no-Wodate. During the festivities, the two princes were commanded to dance; and after first Prince Oke had danced, Prince Woke arose and pronounced this house-blessing* (muro-hogi) *formula.*

89
The ropes of the young *muro* house built up,
The pillars built up
    Are the mainstay of the heart of the lord
        of this house.
The beams laid in place
    Are the flourishing of the heart of the lord
        of this house.
The rafters laid in place
    Are the setting in order of the heart of the lord
        of this house.
The crosspieces laid in place
    Are the levelness of the heart of the lord
        of this house.
The ropes tied in place
    Are the firm securing of the life of the lord
        of this house.
The grass thatched on the roof
    Is the abundance of the wealth of the lord
        of this house.
Izumo is newly cultivated;

The ten-span rice ears
         of the newly cultivated fields
Have been distilled to wine
         in shallow vessels;
Partake thereof with pleasure,
Oh my lads.

As I dance,
Lifting up the horns
Of a deer of these hills—
You cannot buy such as this
In the market of Wega
         of the tasty wine!
So clap your hands heartily,
My eternal ones!

Following the preceding house-blessing formula, Prince Woke sang this song, which delighted Wodate the governor, who asked for more. Then Prince Woke performed a dance and revealed his identity, whereupon Wodate left his seat and made obeisance.

90   The willow
        Growing by the river—
        As the water flows,
        It bends, then rises up,
        But does not lose its roots.

Sung on the first day of the New Year.

91   At the beginning
        Of the new year—
        In this manner,
        Let us for a thousand years
        Enjoy these pleasures!

When Empress Shōtoku went in 770 A.D. to visit the palace of Yugi in Kawachi, the young men and women of six immigrant families (i.e., Chinese and Korean), numbering in all 230 people, lined up in rows and performed an utagaki dance. This was the song first performed.

92   The maidens,
        Lined up opposite the youths,
        Stamp level the ground
        Of the capital in the West—
        The palace of eternal ages!

Following the preceding song, this song was sung among the utagaki songs. The other four songs were all old songs and are not recorded.

93   Its depths and shallow pools
        Are pure and refreshing—
        The Hakata river
        Will continue to be clear
        For a thousand years hence.

Believed to be a song sung in religious ceremonies praying for an abundant harvest. The words are quite difficult of interpretation.

94   The rice ears
        In front of the god
        Of *yū* cloth hanging—
        Oh hang down all together!
        Without anything in particular.

Songs Praising Persons or Gods

When the god Aji-shiki-Taka-hikone came to the funeral of the god Ame-no-wakahiko, he was mistaken for the deceased god by the parents and widow of the deceased. Incensed that he was taken for a dead man, Aji-shiki-Taka-hikone drew his sword and cut down the funeral house, which he kicked away. As he was about to leave, his younger sister sang this song of praise for him.

95   Ah, the large bead
           Strung on the cord of beads
           Worn around the neck
           Of the heavenly
           Young weaving maiden.

           Like this is he
           Who crosses
           Two valleys at once,
           The god Aji-shiki-
           Taka-hikone.

The Kuzu of Yoshino, seeing the sword worn by Prince Ō-sazaki (later Emperor Nintoku), sang this song.

96   Ō-sazaki,
           Ō-sazaki,
           Sun-prince
           Of Homuda—
           The sword which you wear
           Is worn as a sword at the hilt,
           But the end of the scabbard is shaking
           Like a small shrub
           Growing at the leafless trunk
           Of a winter tree.
           Saya saya!

Sung by Iwa-no-hime, Empress of Emperor Nintoku, in 342 A.D. as she sailed up the river towards Yamashiro after refusing to return to the Emperor's palace, jealous at the news that he had wedded Princess Yata.

97   As I ascend,
     As I ascend the river,
   The Yamashiro river
     Of many mountain peaks,
   By the bank of the river
     There is growing
   A *sashibu*
     A *sashibu* tree.
   Underneath it
     There is growing
   A wide-leaved
     Sacred camellia tree.
   Like its flowers,
     Shining brilliantly,
   Like its leaves,
     Wide and calm
   Are you, my great lord.

Directly after song 88, the Kojiki *records this song as sung by the Empress of Emperor Yūryaku.*

98   In this high place
            Of Yamato,
        In the slightly elevated
            Market place,

        By the Hall of the New Grain
            There grows
        A wide-leaved
            Sacred camellia tree.
        Like its leaves,
            You are wide and calm;
        Like its flowers,
            You shine brilliantly—
        Oh to the high-shining
            Prince of the Sun,
        Present
            The abundant wine!

        These are
        The words,
        The words handed down.

Wodo-hime presented this song to Emperor Yūryaku.

99   My great lord,
            Ruling in peace,
        Each morning
            Leans upon,
        Each evening
            Leans upon
        His arm-rest—would that I were
            Even the bottom board of it!
        Oh my brother!

In 468 A.D., Emperor Yūryaku commanded a carpenter to build a high building. An uneme *(court serving lady), watching the nimble movements of the carpenter on the high building, suddenly fell down in the courtyard. The Emperor suspected that the carpenter had violated the* uneme *and turned him over to be executed. Hata-no-Sake-no-kimi, seeking to make the Emperor understand the innocence of the carpenter by music, played the* koto *and said these words. The Emperor, understanding the voice of the* koto, *pardoned the carpenter.*

100   Hanging up for endless years
The flourishing branches
Of the field of Ise,
Of Ise
Of the divine wind—
Until they are gone,
Would that my life
Were also this long,
That my lord
Faithfully
I might serve—
Ah, thus said the carpenter,
Oh pity the poor carpenter!

On the seventh day of the New Year of 612 A.D., Empress Suiko held a banquet, at which Soga-no-Umako, the contemporary Prime Minister, sang this song.

101
    Our great lord
        Is hidden
    Within the myriad rays of heaven;
        When we see
    Her emerge
        From the heavens, we wish:
    For ten thousand ages,
        May it be thus;
    For a thousand ages,
        May it be thus;
    For a thousand ages,
        May it be thus;
    That fearfully
        We might serve her;
    That worshipfully
        We might serve her.
    We present tribute in song.

In reply to the previous song, Empress Suiko sang this song in praise of the Soga clan.

102
    Oh Ma-soga!
        The lads of Soga,
    Were they horses,
        Would be steeds of Himuka;
    Were they swords,
        True blades of Kure.
    True it is
        That the lads of Soga
    Are employed
        By the Emperor.

The following two songs were sung at a banquet given by Emperor Shōmu in 743 A.D.

103   The grandchild
         Of the heavenly deities
         Takes in his hands
         And awesomely consumes
         This abundant wine.

104   Our great lord,
         Ruling in peace,
         Calm of heart
         And long of life,
         Consumes the abundant wine.

Songs Praising Lands or Countries

Songs 105–107 are attributed to different authors in the Kojiki *and* Nihon Shoki. *The* Kojiki *has it that they were sung in 110 A.D. by Yamato Takeru shortly before his death when he arrived at the plain of Nobo in the land of Ise and yearned for his homeland.*
  The Nihon Shoki *attributes them to Emperor Keikō during his royal visit to Kyūshū in 87 A.D., when he came to the moor of Nime in Hyūga.*

105 Yamato
Is the highest part of the land;
The mountains are green partitions
Lying layer upon layer.
Nestled among the mountains,
How beautiful is Yamato!

106 Youths,
Sure of long life,
Take white oak leaves
From the Heguri mountains
(Of the rush matting)
And wear them in your hair,
Oh you youths!

107 From the direction
Of my beloved home
The clouds are rising.

Attributed in the Kinkafu *to Emperor Keikō (reigned traditionally 71–130 A.D.), who sang it in the land of Himuka (probably present Hyūga in Kyūshū), yearning for the palace in Yamato.*

108   The sky-full
     Land of Yamato—
     Is it because of its divinity?—
     Is an ideal land to be in;
     Is it because of its landside?—
     Is an ideal place to live in.
     The ideal land
     Is the Dragon-fly Island, Yamato.

When Emperor Ōjin visited the land of Afumi (Ōmi) in 275 A.D., he arrived at the plain of Uji and looked out at the plain of Kazu, singing this song.

109   When I view
     The Kazu plain
     Of the myriad leaves,
     The prospering villages are visible;
     The highest part of the land is visible.

In 462 A.D., Emperor Yūryaku visited the moor of Hatsuse, viewed the aspect of the mountains and moors, and sang this song in an outburst of feeling.

110   The mountain of Hatsuse
               Of the hidden country
        Is a mountain
               Standing beautifully,
        Is a mountain
               Projecting beautifully.
        The mountain of Hatsuse
               Of the hidden country
        Is truly lovely,
               Is truly lovely.

On the fifth day of the fifth month of 743 A.D., Emperor Shōmu gave a banquet, at which the Crown Princess, the later Empress Kōken, danced the Go-sechi *dance (see song 80). Thereupon the Emperor made this song.*

111   The sky-full
        Land of Yamato,
        Because of its divinity,
        Must be holy indeed—
        So do I think when seeing this dance.

Songs Praising Palaces

The god Susa-no-wo, after having subjugated the eight-headed dragon, took as his bride Princess Kushinata and arrived at Suga in the land of Izumo, where he decided to build his palace, and sang this song.

112   Oh, the many-fenced palace
In Izumo of the rising clouds!
To live therein with my spouse,
I build a many-fenced palace.
Oh, that many-fenced palace!

Emperor Keikō in 88 A.D. visited a place called Mikè in Tsukushi in Kyūshū. There was a fallen tree 970 rods in length over which the court officials passed as if it were a bridge. The contemporaries made this song.

113   The bridge of Mikè
Of the morning frost—
The court nobles
Cross over it—
The bridge of Mikè.

(Following songs 88 and 98, in that order.) Emperor Yūryaku sang this song. After the feast, he praised the uneme *of Mie and rewarded her with many presents.*

114   The courtiers
     Of the great palace
   Like quails,
     Donning their scarves,
   Like wagtails,
     Their tails criss-crossing,
   Like garden sparrows,
     Bowing low,
   Today also seem
     To be steeped in wine,
   The high-shining
     Sun palace courtiers.

   These are
   The words,
   The words handed down.

After the death of Emperor Seinei in the first month of 484 A.D., both Prince Oke and his younger brother Prince Woke ceded the throne to each other and each refused to assume the dignity for himself. During the interregnum their sister, Princess Awo of Ii-toyo, ruled the country in the Palace of Tsunusashi in Oshinumi. A contemporary poet made this song.

115   In Yamato
   That which is good to see
   Is this high building
   Of Oshinumi—
   The palace of Tsunusashi.

WINE-PRAISING AND DRINKING SONGS

Emperor Sūjin appointed Ō-tata-neko as priest to the god Ō-mono-nushi and caused him to worship the god on the 20th day of the 12th month of 90 B.C. at Ōmiwa. At this time Ikuhi of Takahashi, who had that year been appointed as Brewer to the god, presented sacred wine to the Emperor and sang this song, after which a feast was held in the shrine of the god.

116   This wine
           Is not my wine.
       It is wine
           Distilled by Ō-mono-nushi,
           Who builds Yamato.

       Many long years!
       Many long years!

When the Prince Imperial Homuda (later Emperor Ōjin) returned to Yamato from Tsunaga in 213 A.D., his mother, Empress Jingū, brewed wine to augur his safe return (machi-zake) *and presenting the wine to him, sang this song.*

117   This wine
               Is not my wine;
         It is wine which
         The ruler of wine,
               He who dwells in the Eternal World,
         The rock-standing
               God Sukuna,
         Divinely blessed,
               Blessed with fury,
         Abundantly blessed,
               Blessed going around,
         And presented.
         Drink deeply.
               Sa sa!

In reply to the preceding song, Takeshi-Uchi-no-sukune made this song on behalf of Prince Homuda.

118   Whoever it was
         Who distilled this wine
         Must have distilled it
         Turning his drum
         On one side for a mortar,
         While singing songs;
         He must have distilled it
         While dancing.
         That must be why this wine,
         This wine
         Is so extraordinarily enjoyable.
               Sa sa!

During the reign of Emperor Ōjin (traditionally 270–310 A.D.), a man called Niho, also called Susukori, came to Japan as an immigrant. Susukori, who was skilled at distilling wine, offered wine to the Emperor, who greatly rejoiced in the liquor and sang this song.

119   I have become drunk
On the wine distilled
By Susukori;
I have become drunk
On this wine of peace,
This wine of laughter.

The Hitachi Fudoki *records this song as being sung traditionally by the men and women of the priestly Urabe family of the Kashima Shrine in Hitachi. At the time of the festival of the shrine on the 10th day of the 4th month every year, the members of the Urabe family engaged in a day and night celebration, feasting, singing, and dancing.*

120   The newly brewed
Wine of the god—
Because I was told
To drink it,
I have become drunk.

The Kojiki *records this song directly after song 96, with the following account. Again, the* Kuzu *of Yoshino, making a long slender mortar, presented wine to the Emperor. Clacking their mouths, they sang and danced when performing this song, which is sung by them down to the present day when they present their local produce at the Court.*

121   Where the oak trees are growing,
                We made a long slender mortar,
                And in this mortar
                We brewed this excellent wine;
                Partake of it
                With pleasure,
                Oh my father!

Following song 114, the Kojiki *records this song with the following narrative. On the day of this feast, Wodo-hime of Kasuga presented wine to Emperor Yūryaku, who sang this song. (Then Wodo-hime replied with song 99.)*

122   (The spraying water)
                    Court noble maiden
                Holds the large wine-jug.
                Holding the large wine-jug,
                    Oh hold it firmly,
                Firmly from the bottom,
                    Ever more firmly hold it,
                    Oh, girl holding the large wine-jug!

Buddhist Religious Songs

The 23 songs contained in this section are the oldest Buddhist verse in the Japanese Language.

The first twenty songs (songs 123–142) are carved on a stone tablet preserved today at Yakushi-ji Temple in Nara in a little building which also houses the famous large stone on which are carved replicas of the foot-prints of Sakyamuni Buddha. These foot-prints were carved on stone around the year 752 A.D. by order of a nobleman of the highest birth, Chinu (later Jōsan), who lived in the late *Manyō* era and died in 770 A.D.

Because of the wording of the songs themselves, it is highly probable that these twenty songs were authored by Chinu himself in commemoration of the carving of the foot-print stone. But the last four songs (139–142), which are preceded by a heading meaning something like "Reprimands on Life and Death," differ conspicuously in mood and content from the others and probably were composed on a different occasion.

These twenty songs are all written in a uniform verse form having 6 lines of 5-7-5-7-7-7 syllables, respectively—because this verse form is associated most closely with the songs on this tablet, it has been modernly named the *Bussoku-seki-ka tai*, the "Buddha's foot-print stone song style." With a few noteworthy exceptions, the final 7-syllable line is usually merely a repetition, with minor variations in wording, of the fifth line. For this reason, this verse form has been called a mere variation of the *tanka*.

Here and there in this volume there are other songs (for example, songs 182, 184, and 235) which can be explained as being in this same verse form. There are also traces of it in the *Manyōshū* and in older examples of *wasan*, the Buddhist hymns in Japanese. It is a verse form which has always been closely connected with songs actually meant to be sung.

The final three songs (143–145) are recorded in the *Tōdaiji Yōroku* as songs which were sent by Gangoji Temple to Tōdaiji temple when the giant statue of Vairocana Buddha was dedicated there in the year 752 A.D. Thus these three songs are also contemporary with the preceding twenty songs.

123 Oh let the reverberations from this rock
On which are being carved the holy foot-prints
Reach to the heavens
And cause the very earth to shake—
For the sake of our fathers and mothers,
For the sake of all men.

124 The site where trod
The man endowed abundantly
With thirty
And two beautiful forms
And eighty lovely appearances—
How precious it is!

125 Unable, I, to see
Even the prints of the feet
Which were seen with their own eyes
By the holy men of old,
I carve their form upon a rock,
I carve their form upon a jewel.

126 Would that these holy foot-prints
Unleash eighty thousand
Streams of light,
And bring salvation to all men!
Would that they ferry them across!
Would that they bring salvation to them!

127   What kind
       Of man must it have been
       To have trod
       Upon a rock as upon the earth
       And to have left a foot-print thereon?
       Ah how holy this!

128   Let us recall him reverently
       As we see these foot-prints of the steps
       Trod by the intrepid hero
       Who walked ahead—
       Until we meet him directly,
       Until we meet him face to face.

129   The prints of the steps
       Trod by the intrepid hero
       Remain still now
       Upon the rock,
       Bidding: "Looking upon this, remember me,
       For ever more remember me."

130   Following in the path
       Of these holy foot-prints,
       To the land where dwell
       The holy men
       Let me also go,
       Bringing with me all men.

131   Copying on a rock
The holy foot-prints of Sakya,
Let us reverence them,
And to the latter-day Buddha,
Let us hand them on,
Let us present them as an offering.

132   Even though this age
Changes and departs,
May you remain
In all eternity,
For the sake of latter ages,
For the sake of the ages to come.

133   Oh company blessed
With happy fortune!
How enviable those
Who came
And saw with their own eyes.
Ah what happiness!

134   Miserable as I am,
There are many
Still lower than I.
That these may be ferried across,
I have copied these foot-prints,
I have made these foot-prints.

135   Copying down on a stone
             The foot-prints of Sakya,
             Going around them,
             Revering them,
             I would spend my life,
             I would spend this life.

136   There are
             The usual healers;
             But this rare guest,
             The newly arrived healer,
             How holy he is,
             How rare he is!

137   As we reverently circle
             Round these holy foot-prints,
             Of the jewel-like appearance
             Of their maker
             Are we reminded:
             It is as if we could see him.

138   Those who come
             To see the sacred foot-prints—
             Their sins of the past,
             Even of a thousand past ages,
             Will vanish, so it is said,
             Will be taken away, so I hear.

139   Because of all beings,
It is most difficult to be born as a man,
This life is given as a means
For acquiring the law.
Exert yourselves, all men!
Go forward, all men!

140   This unclean body,
Composed of
The four serpents
And the five ghosts,
Is to be detested and cast away,
Is to be shunned and cast away.

141   This body,
Evanescent like a flash
Of lightning,
Is forever accompanied
By the Great King of Death.
Should we not tremble with fear?

142   On behalf of those
Wandering perplexed
In this world,
We seek a healer,
We seek a holy man,
In order to awaken them.

The three songs sent by Gangoji Temple to the dedication of the Great Buddha at Tōdaiji Temple in 752 A.D.

143 We present flowers
To the Buddha Rusana,
Who has chosen as his site
The foot-hills to the East
For their purity.

144 The source of the Law
Has here come to full bloom.
From today on,
The Law of the Buddha
Will continue to flourish.

145 We present songs
From the temple of Asuka
Of the flying birds,
Where first arose
The spring of the Law.

Elegies

This section contains several songs about which there has been some doubt. I have in general been rather conservative, accepting as *bona fide* elegies most of the songs which are plainly so labeled in the prose narratives.

The elegy reaches the height of its development with the *Manyōshū*; the ancient elegies in this section cannot compare, at least in quantity, with those of the *Manyō* poets. However, there are some which show fine feeling and superior literary value.

When the illness of the hero Yamato Takeru became grave, he sang this song. After he finished singing it, he died. (According to the Nihon Shoki, *this was in 113 A.D.)*

146   Ah, the sword
                 Which I left
                 By the maiden's
                 Sleeping place—
                 Alas, that sword!

When news of the demise of Yamato Takeru reached Yamato, his wives and children all came down and constructed his tomb; and, crawling around in the rice paddy bordering on the tomb, sang this song in tears.

147   Like the vines of the *tokoro* roots,
                 We crawl around
                 Among the rice stems,
                 The rice stems in the field
                 Bordering on the tomb.

(Following the preceding song.) Here the soul of Yamato Takeru turned into a huge white bird and went flying through the sky towards the beach. His wives and children, paying no heed to the pain caused when their feet were injured by the stumps of the bamboo reeds, chased after the bird in tears. This is the song they sang at the time.

148   Moving with difficulty, up to our waists
     In the field of low bamboo plants;
     We cannot go through the sky—
     But, alas, must go by foot!

The song sung by the wives and children of Yamato Takeru when they entered the sea water and moved forward with difficulty after the white bird.

149   Going by sea, our waists in the water,
     We move forward with difficulty;
     Like plants growing
     By a large river,
     We drift aimlessly
     In the ocean currents.

The song sung by the wives and children of Yamato Takeru when the bird flew and landed on the rocky shores.

150   Like the plovers of the beach,
     We do not go by the sandy beaches,
     But follow along the rocky shores.

When the corpse of Prince Ō-yama-mori (who had been killed after his plot to murder Prince Uji had backfired) came to the surface of the water, Prince Uji sang this song.

151 The *azusa* tree, the *mayumi* tree
    Standing by the shallow ford,
  The ford of Uji
    Of the dauntless men:

  Although my heart wishes
    To cut them down,
  Although my heart wishes
    To take them,

  At the lower part of the trees
    I recall my lord;
  At the tips of the branches
    I recall my beloved;

  Impatiently,
    I think of this;
  Lovingly,
    I think of that—

  And come back without cutting down
  The *azusa* tree, the *mayumi* tree.

(After song 55.) Emperor Muretsu, realizing that Shibi had already possessed Kage-hime, sent troops to kill Shibi, who met his death at Mt. Nara. At this time, Kage-hime, who had gone along with Shibi, saw him being killed, and sang this song tearfully, overwhelmed by sorrow.

152   Passing Furu
     Of Isu-no-kami,
   Passing Takahashi
     Of the straw pillow,
   Passing Ōyake
     Of the many treasures,
   Passing Kasuga
     Of the spring day,
   Passing Wosaho
     Of the hidden wife—
   With a beautiful bowl
     Filled with rice,
   With a beautiful cup
     Filled with water,
   She goes, wet with tears,
     Alas, poor Kage-hime!

(Following the preceding song.) After hurriedly burying Shibi, Kage-hime, choking with sorrow, said as she was about to depart for home: "Ah, how painful! This day I have lost my dearest husband!" Then, shedding tears of irrepressible grief, she sang this song.

153   Hidden like a wild animal
   In the watery place
   In the ravine
   Of Nara mountain—
   Lies the youth Shibi
   (Of the spraying water)—
   Oh do not search him out,
   You wild boars!

In 530 A.D., Kena-no-omi, Japanese resident in Mimana (Imna, the Japanese colony in Korea), was relieved of his duties and summoned back. He died when he reached the island of Tsushima. As his funeral procession proceeded up the Yodo river towards Afumi (Ōmi), his wife sang this song.

154   Past Hirakata
            He ascends playing a flute—
            The youth Kena
            Of Afumi
            Ascends playing a flute.

On the 22nd day of the New Year of 622 A.D., Prince Shōtoku was taken ill. The Prince's consort, Lady Kashiwade, also became ill because of fatigue. On the 21st day of the second month, the consort died, and on the following day the Prince himself died. When Lady Kashiwade was about to die, she asked for water. The Prince would not permit it. Finally after the Lady died, the Prince made this elegy.

155   Water of the well of Tomi
            Of Ikaruga—
            Since she was not to live,
            Would that I had presented it to her—
            Water of the well of Tomi!

Songs 156–158 are three elegies supposedly written by someone called Kose-no-Mitsue on the death of Prince Shōtoku (died in 622 A.D.).

156   If the Tomi river
                  Of Ikaruga should cease to flow—
                  Only then
                  Would the name of our great lord
                  Be forgotten.

157   Alas, my great lord,
                  You who were spoken of
                  As being in the shade of the *aji* tree
                  Of Mount Tabasami,
                  The domain of the god.

158   On these partition-like mountains
                  Around Ikaruga grow trees
                  Towering into the skies:
                  Would that I could say about you, my lord,
                  That this, too, was as empty as the skies.

Soga-no-Miyatsuko-hime, consort of the Prince Imperial (later Emperor Tenchi) died of a broken heart in 648 A.D. after her father had been killed as the result of slander. The Prince grieved deeply at her death. Nonaka-no-Kawara-no-Fuhito-Maro came forward and presented these songs.

159   On the mountain stream
       Is a pair of mandarin ducks—
       Well matched like them
       Were my beloved and I—
       But who has led her away?

Second elegy by Nonaka-no-Kawara-no-Fuhito-Maro. The Prince praised the songs highly and, giving a koto *to the scribe, had him sing the songs. He also rewarded him richly with gifts.*

160   On each stem
       Flowers are blooming;
       But why
       Will my dear beloved
       Never bloom forth again?

In 658 A.D., Prince Takeru, the grandson of Empress Saimei, died at the age of eight and was interred in a tomb above the Imaki valley. The Empress, beside herself with grief, commanded that he be interred along with her after her own death and made three songs which she sang from time to time as she lamented bitterly.

161 Above the hill
At Imaki—
If even a cloud
Would only appear,
Then what should I grieve?

162 I did not think of him
As being a mere child, young
Like the young grass
By the river bank, where they track
The wounded deer.

163 Like the foaming waters
Of the Asuka river,
Moving on ceaselessly:
Without pause
Does my mind dwell on him.

In the winter of 658 A.D.—after her grandson Prince Takeru had died that summer—Empress Saimei went to the hotspring at Ki (modern Wakayama prefecture). Remembering her lost grandson, she grieved and lamented, singing these three songs.
Songs 164–166 are a sequence of laments, all closely interwoven.

164   Though I cross the mountains
And sail over the seas,
I shall not forget
The happy
Times in Imaki.

165   The salt current
At the river mouth
Flows back into the sea:
With darkness at my back,
Must I go, leaving him behind?

166   Must I go,
Leaving behind
My beloved young child?

After Empress Saimei died at the Palace of Asakura in Kyūshū in 661 A.D.,
her son the Prince Imperial (later Emperor Tenchi), anchoring his ship at a certain place,
remained there to mourn for the Empress. He broke into song and sang this.

167 Because of my yearning
  To see your form,
  Must I remain anchored here
  And yearn thus?—
  Wishing to see your form . . .

The priest Shingon, a former local lord who had entered the religious life,
was a disciple of the saintly priest Gyōki (d. 749). Shingon had sworn to die and go to
Paradise together with Gyōki, but unfortunately died before Gyōki. Thereupon, Gyōki tearfully
made this song.

168 That old liar bird,
  The crow—
  In words only
  You said we would go together,
  But you went on ahead.

War Songs

This section contains twelve songs which, in my judgment, are chiefly on martial themes; this is a category which does not occur in later Japanese poetry and is unique with the ancient songs.

Particularly interesting are the *Kume-uta* (songs 169–175), war songs traditionally connected with the Kume clan of warriors, most of which end with the words "*Uchite shi yamamu*"—which words (usually translated here as "we will smite them utterly") were revived, some 1200 years later, as a slogan during the Second World War.

According to the Kojiki, *this song was sung by Emperor Jimmu as a signal for his men to strike at the enemy (warriors of the race called Tsuchi-gumo) who had been lured to a banquet.*

169
　　Many people
　　　　Are in the large
　　Muro house
　　　　Of Osaka.
　　Even though many people
　　　　Are there,
　　The gallant
　　　　Lads of Kume
　　With their tomahawks,
　　　　With their stone mallets,
　　Will smite them utterly!

　　The gallant
　　　　Lads of Kume,
　　With their tomahawks,
　　　　With their stone mallets—
　　Now is the time to strike!

After the men had heard the preceding song and had slain all the enemy, they greatly rejoiced and, looking up towards the heavens, laughed, singing this song.

The Nihon Shoki *adds that this is the origin of the practice of the Kume clan who today still laugh loudly after they have sung this song.*

170   Ah, now it is!
               Ah, now it is!
               A a si ya wo!
               Now at last,
               My lads!
               Now at last,
               My lads!

Again they sang this song.

171   People say
               That one Emishi
               Is a match for a hundred men;
               But they did not even rcsist.

The Kojiki *attributes songs 172–174 to Emperor Jimmu, who supposedly sang them when about to strike an enemy called Tomibiko.*

172   In the millet field
Of the gallant
Lads of Kume:
A single smelling leek—
Up with it by its roots,
With all the buds on its roots:
Thus we will utterly extirpate them!

173   Beneath the fence
Of the gallant
Lads of Kume,
Grows a pepper plant—
It burns the mouth;
Like this sting, I will not forget,
But will smite them utterly!

174   On the large rocks
Of the sea of Ise
Of the divine wind,
There are crawling around
Shell-fish,
Shell-fish—
     Oh my lads, oh my lads—
Like the shell-fish,
Crawling around them,
We will smite them utterly!
We will smite them utterly!

Sung by Emperor Jimmu when his ever victorious army had become ex-hausted while fighting E-shiki and Oto-shiki of Yamato.

175   Watching the enemy
      While going through the woods
      Of Mount Inasa
      Of the lined-up shields,
      We fought,
      But now we are starving.
      Oh birds of the islands,
      Oh clan of Cormorant Keepers,
      Come quickly to our aid!

During the reign of Empress Jingū, when the general Takeshi-Uchi-no-sukune was about to engage in battle the rebel Prince Oshikuma (this was traditionally in 201 A.D.), someone called Kuma-no-kori went to the vanguard of Prince Oshikuma's army and sang this song loudly in order to urge on the men.

176   Going across the river
       To the sparse pine forest yonder,
     To the pine forest,
       To their bows
    Of *tsuki* wood
       Fixing knob-headed arrows,

     The nobles
       Together with other nobles,
     Intimate friends
       With intimate friends,

     Come, let us fight,
       I say!
     Inside the belly
       Of the lord of Uchi

     Of the jewel-cutting,
       Are there grains of sand?
     No, so let us fight,
       I say!

Prince Oshikuma, defeated in battle, fled with his general, Isahi (in the Nihon Shoki, Isachi)-no-sukune. After singing this song, they jumped from their boat into the sea of Afumi (lake Biwa). Furu-kuma was the general of Empress Jingū's army.

177   Come, my lad,
     Rather than receive the wounds
       Inflicted by Furu-kuma,
     Come, like the *niho* birds,
       Let us die here, diving into the waters
       Of the lake of Afumi!

After Oshikuma had dived into the waters, Takeshi-Uchi-no-sukune sang this song.

178   The bird which dived
     Into the ford of Seta
     Of the lake of Afumi
     Is not visible to the eye,
     And how angry I am!

After several days, the bodies of Prince Oshikuma and his general were discovered at Uji. At this time Takeshi-Uchi-no-sukune made this song.

179   The bird which dived
     Into the ford of Seta
     Of the lake of Afumi
     Has passed by Tanakami
     And was caught at Uji.

In 479 A.D., Woshiro, ruler of Kibi, general of the expedition against Silla in Korea, arrived at his homeland, Kibi. 500 Emishi under his command rebelled, and Woshiro quelled them all single-handed. Having run out of arrows, he took his bow in his hand and sang this song, then proceeded to kill all the rebels.

180   The lad Woshiro,
           Fighting on the road!
        Although his mother
           May not hear of it,
        At least may his countrymen
           Hear of it!

Popular Songs

In this section I have included many of the songs which were handed down and sung among the general populace. In some cases—particularly in the folk song section—there is no conclusive proof that a song was or was not popular; however, I was careful in consulting the views of all native authorities before assigning any songs here. Popular songs dealing with various aspects of love have been included in the section for Love Songs.

I have distinguished two categories: Folk Songs and Satirical Songs.

The Satirical Songs include mostly *waza-uta*, those strange, often weird songs which suddenly came—seemingly from nowhere—and appeared in the mouths of the people and to which the compilers of the *Nihon Shoki* attributed prophetic meanings. It is strange that so few Japanese scholars have noticed the political protest which is so obvious in many of these *waza-uta*.

FOLK SONGS

After Emperor Jimmu had defeated E-ukashi, the chief of the Uda district, because of the defection of Oto-ukashi, the younger brother of E-ukashi, the Emperor distributed to his army the banquet presented by Oto-ukashi and sang this song.

181   On the high place
Of Uda,
We set a snipe-net;
We waited,
But no snipe were caught.
Instead,
A whale was caught.

If the first wife
Asks for some to eat,
Cut off and give her
Only a little, like the berries
Of the *tachi-soba.*

But if the second wife
Asks for some to eat,
Cut off and give her
Plenty, like the berries
Of the *ichi-sakaki!*

    Ee si ya ko si ya!
    Aa si ya ko si ya!

When the hero Yamato Takeru came to the Cape of Wotsu in the land of Ise and found at the foot of a lone pine there a sword which he had forgotten on a previous occasion, he sang this song.

182   Oh lone pine
            Standing on the cape of Wotsu
            Directly opposite
            Wohari—
                    Oh my brother!—
            Oh lone pine,
            If you were a man,
            I would give you a sword to wear,
            I would dress you with clothes,
            Oh lone pine—
                    Oh my brother!

This song is found in a fragment of the Ise Fudoki *quoted in the* Manyō-shū Chūshaku, *a commentary on the* Manyōshū *compiled in 1269 by the priest Sengaku. It is attributed to Emperor Keikō (reigned traditionally 71–130 A.D.) when he visited the place called Mato-kata in the land of Ise.*

183   The valiant warriors
            Fix to their bows lucky arrows,
            Stand opposite,
            And shoot at Mato-kata, which
            Has a beach truly pure and refreshing.

Recorded in the Harima Fudoki *as a song about the plain of Wome in the land of Harima. The wording of the prose narrative is not clear on this point, but it is possible that the intention was to attribute the song to Emperor Ōjin (reigned traditionally 270–310 A.D.) when he visited the place.*

184   Even though
On the lovable leaves
Of the bamboo-grass of Wome,
The hail and frost should fall;
Yet do not wither,
Oh bamboo-grass of Wome!

The Kinkafu *contains three accounts of this song's origins, none of which seems to fit the words of the song very well.*

The first account attributes it to Emperor Nintoku while going from Mt. Heguri to Mt. Yata (both mountains in Nara Prefecture) to see Princess Yata (see also songs 42–43), whom he was prevented from introducing into the Palace as his concubine by the jealousy of the Empress.

The second account is that the song was made by Empress Jingū when she crossed Mt. Nara and looked towards Kazuraki.

The third account says that the Kojiki attributes this song to a contemporary of Emperor Ōjin. A contemporary sang it when Emperor Ōjin went hunting. However, the song does not appear at all in the Kojiki.

185   The little bamboo of Mihara
Of Awaji,
The island-country—
I pulled up by the roots,
Pulled up and brought,
And planted
By the spring
Of Asatsuma.
The little bamboo of Mihara
Of Awaji!

Recorded in a fragment of the Hizen Fudoki *quoted in the* Manyōshū
Chūshaku.

*The account is as follows: Mt. Kishima is a solitary mountain in Kishima
County in the land of Hizen (modern Saga Prefecture, Kyūshū). The local men and women
climb it every year in spring and autumn, bringing wine and* koto, *and disport themselves in
feasting, singing, and dancing. These are the words of the song they sing.*

186   Losing hold of the grass
          On the rugged slopes
          Of mount Kishima
          Of the falling hail,
          I take hold of my beloved's hand.

*An intrigue developed between Princess Medori (half-sister of Emperor
Nintoku) and Prince Hayabusa-wake (younger brother of the Emperor). The Emperor,
enraged at their provocations, raised troops to kill them. Then Prince Hayabusa-wake and
Princess Medori fled and climbed Mt. Kurahashi (in Nara Prefecture). At this time Prince
Hayabusa-wake sang this song.*

187   Losing hold of the crags
          On the rugged slopes
          Of ladder-steep
          Mount Kurahashi—
          Ah, she takes my hand!

(Following the preceding song.) Again, Prince Hayabusa-wake sang this song.

188

Though ladder-like
Mount Kurahashi
Is steep,
Now that I climb it with my beloved,
It seems not steep at all.

Attributed in the Nihon Shoki *also to Prince Hayabusa-wake when he fled with Princess Medori and crossed Mt. Soni (rather than Mt. Kurahashi).*

The incidents recorded in connection with songs 187–189 occurred, according to the Nihon Shoki, *in the year 352 A.D.*

189

The mountain,
Steep as a ladder—
Now that I cross it
Together with my beloved,
Is like a soft carpet.

Recorded in the Kojiki *as the second song sung by the old woman Hiketa-no-Aka-iko to Emperor Yūryaku (see songs 52, 77–78).*

190

In the bay of Kusaka
Grow lotuses of the bay,
Flowering lotuses:
The thriving youths—
How I envy them.

*Iruka, the son of Soga-no-Emishi, plotted to kill the sons of Prince Shōtoku,
who finally fled and killed themselves to avoid a civil war. This is a* waza-uta *of the time
(643* A.D.*) which was believed to allude to these events.*

191   On top of a boulder
      The monkeys are cooking rice.
      At any rate, have some of the rice
      Before you leave,
      Old man antelope!

*Recorded in two biographies of Prince Shōtoku—which also record song
191. Both accounts agree that this song, together with song 191, predicted the ruin of the
descendants of Prince Shōtoku.*

192   Oh leaves of the *ude* plant
      Of Yamashiro!
      Appear to each other
      As water and metal!
      Oh leaves of the *ude* plant!

This is the first of three waza-uta *which appeared in 644* A.D. *(For a
full account, see songs 59–60.)*
*Shima was the location of the Soga clan, and this song was interpreted as
foretelling their downfall.*

193   From far away
      A *koto* is heard
      In the jungle field of Shima.

The first of three waza-uta *(songs 194, 208, 62) which appeared at the time of the death of Emperor Tenchi on the third day of the 12th month of the year 671* A.D.

These three songs were interpreted as applying to the delicate situation which followed Emperor Tenchi's demise, when the Heir Apparent, Prince Ō-ama, the younger brother of the late Emperor, sensing danger to himself, renounced the world and retired to Mt. Yoshino, from which place he secretly raised an army and attained the throne by force. He was the next Emperor, Temmu (reigned 673–686 A.D.*).*

194
        I am a trout,
        A trout of Yeshino.
        A trout should be
        Near a scenic bank.

        Ah, how painful it is here
        Under the *nagi*
        And the *seri* plants!
        Ah, how painful for me!

According to the Shoku Nihongi, *the song was sung everywhere in the country before the coronation of Prince Shirakabe as Emperor Kōjin in 770 A.D., which event it was believed to have foretold.*

195   In front of the temple
Of Katsuragi,
To the West
Of the temple of Toyora—

     Oshitodo
     Toshotodo

In the Sakura Spring
Lie submerged white jewels,
Lie submerged precious jewels—

     Oshitodo
     Toshitodo

If thus it is,
The land will prosper,
My house will prosper—

     Oshitodo
     Toshitodo

During the second reign of Empress Kōken (under the name of Empress Shōtoku, 764–770 A.D.), this waza-uta *was sung everywhere throughout the country. After Prince Yabe became Emperor, under the name of Emperor Kammu, in 781 A.D., this song was regarded as an omen prophesying that Prince Yabe would one day ascend the throne.*

196   The hill of Yabe
                Directly opposite
                Ōmiya—
                Do not tread hard on it,
                Even though it is nothing but earth!

In the year 795 A.D., the year after the palace was moved to the new Heian capital (in present-day Kyōto), Emperor Kammu sang at a banquet this furu-uta.

197   The old path through the fields
                Of long ago—
                If one were to change it,
                It could be changed—
                The old path through the fields.

The following seven songs are without prose narrative.

198   By the roadside
The *hari* and *kunugi* trees
Are being coquettish, *na iyo.*
Are being coquettish, *me ya.*

Are being coquettish,
So it is said—
The *hari* and *kunugi* trees,
The *hari* and *kunugi* trees.

199   The paddy made
By the heavenly ones,
The rocky paddy is no good.
The rocky paddy—
When I make my own,
It sounds *kawara.*
It sounds *yura:*
The rocky paddy is no good,
The rocky paddy is no good.

200   By the river Yamashiro
Of the many mountain peaks,
A dragon-fly sneezes,
A dragon-fly sneezes.

Even though it sneezes,
I will not give up
Until I meet my beloved,
Until I meet my beloved.

201   Oh warbler bird
Standing in the yard—
Situ itu itura—
Awaken me, my beloved!
Should I go to sleep,
Not knowing that dawn has come.
Situ itura—
Awaken me, oh warbler!

202   Picking up acorns—
You can't store them up, you know!
So eat them with pleasure,
Oh my aunty,
And sleep with pleasure!

203   The large sedge field
At the foot of the mountain—
The cows tread on it;

Though the cows
And the boars tread on it—
You, common people, must not tread on it!

204   The river *hari* tree
Up the river—
I am cool towards him, *we ya*,
I am cool towards him—
But since we have been grafted together,
I think of him as a relative.

A song made by contemporaries to praise a man called Kazuno-no-Hata-no-miyatsuko-Kawakatsu, the head of the immigrant family Hata (also called Utsumasa or Uzumasa) whose center was Kazuno.

Around 644 A.D., a man called Ōfube-no-Ō began to propagate the worship of a kind of caterpillar, calling it Tokoyo-no-Kami *(God of the Eternal World) and promising wealth and longevity to those who would worship it. Priests and priestesses conspired with him to deceive the people into believing in this cult, and many evils ensued. Kazuno-no-Hata-no-miyatsuko-Kawakatsu slew Ōfube-no-Ō, thus putting an end to the cult.*

205   Utsumasa
Has truly punished
That which was proclaimed
To be such a mighty god,
The God of the Eternal World.

In 660 A.D., the kingdom of Paekche asked for help from Empress Saimei in its war against the kingdom of Silla. Various omens portended the defeat of the army of relief, and there was this waza-uta.

206   The wild geese are eating
The mountain rice-paddy
Made by
The flat-backed hunchback.

Because the Empress's hunting is neglected,
The wild geese are eating
The mountain rice-paddy.

Because the Empress's words are weak,
The wild geese are eating
The mountain rice-paddy.

In the first month of 671 A.D., Emperor Tenchi granted high ranks to Korean immigrants. At the time there was this waza-uta.

207   The little oranges
       Each grow on separate branches,
       But when strung as beads,
       They are all strung
       On the same cord.

The second of the three waza-uta *which appeared at the time of the death of Emperor Tenchi in 671 A.D. (The other two were songs 194 and 62.)*

208   The court nobles
       Are untying their many cords.
       Before they have untied
       Even one of them,
       The prince unties his cords.

A song sung everywhere throughout the country during the reign of Empress Kōken (749–758 A.D.). Believed to have foretold the death of many princes and courtiers.

209   Oh princes dying young!
       Oh princes dying so lamentably!

       The *todoroki* clam—
           When will it float up to the top?
       The flatfish—
           When will it float up to the top?

The following three songs are recorded in the Nippon Ryōiki *as having been sung everywhere throughout the second reign of Empress Kōken as Empress Shōtoku (764–770 A.D.). They satirize the sexual relations between the Empress and the evil priest Dōkyō.*

210   Do not despise
The Buddhist cleric
For wearing skirts!

Inside them, below the waist-belt,
There hangs a *komo-zuchi*—

And when it finally stands up,
He is a formidable lord, all right!

211   Sleep with my black penis
Between your thighs;
We too are human.

212   Let me meet him face to face.
Underneath the tree,
The reverend cleric,
Puffed with over-eating—
Bring him to me!

Dialogue Songs

Since there are so many question-and-answer, dialogue, and re-partee songs in this collection of verse, I have included them here under this heading.

Besides the songs included here, there are several other songs in two or more parts (such as songs 42–43, 85–87) which could just as well have been included here.

Songs 213–216 are recorded as a song sequence in the Kojiki. *In 661 B.C., Emperor Jimmu sought for a maiden to make his Chief Empress. Ō-kume-no-mikoto recommended the Princess Isukeyori. As the Emperor and Ō-kume-no-mikoto came along the Plain of Takasaji, seven maidens were disporting themselves there; among the maidens was Isukeyori. Ō-kume-no-mikoto, seeing Princess Isukeyori among the maidens, posed this question to the Emperor in a song.*

213   Seven maidens
             Walking along
             The plain of Takasaji
             In Yamato—
             Which of them will you take to wife?

Then the Emperor, knowing in his heart that the maiden in front was Princess Isukeyori, answered with this song.

214   The eldest maiden
             Walking out in front
             I will take to wife.

When Ō-kume-no-mikoto went to announce the Emperor's wishes to Princess Isukeyori, she wondered at his "pierced sharp eyes" and sang this song.

215   *Ametsutsu*
             Chidori mashi toto—
             Why your pierced sharp eyes?

Then Ō-kume-no-mikoto replied with this song. The princess then consented to the Emperor's will.

Ō-kume-no-mikoto had won out in this verbal battle of wits by making a clever reply in the same metrical form as the question. Therefore, the maiden submitted to the Emperor's will.

216   In order the better to meet
               The maidens face to face,
               Are my pierced sharp eyes.

Songs 217–219 are recorded in the Kinkafu *as a song sequence under the name* Ayuda-buri.

The narrative given in the Kinkafu *attributes the three songs to Emperor Keikō (reigned traditionally 71–130 A.D.). When the Empress sent a messenger from Wohari that she was about to give birth to a child, the Emperor sent for her; but the child was born on the way, in the village of Anakui in Kasuga. The Emperor, greatly rejoicing, sang these songs.*

217   Pure water
                   Of the sacred spring of Takahashi—
               You ought
                   To be straight;
               You ought
                   To flow out straight;
               But why are you flowing out
                   In such a place as this?—
               Pure water.

218   In the mountains of Furu
          At Isu-no-kami,
      The bear's claws—
          Does he have six claws?
      The deer's hooves—
          Does he have eight hooves?
      Thinking fondly of you,
          I have come out
      In such a place as this—
          Pure water.

219   Did you pass by
          This morning in the hunt?
      Because I like the post
          At the end of the bridge,
      Because I like the bay
          Between the mountains,
      I have come out
          In such a place as this—
      Pure water.

The first of two question-and-answer songs both in the kata-uta *metrical form. Attributed to the hero Yamato Takeru when he went over from Azuma to the land of Kai. The song was sung while he sojourned at the palace of Sakawori.*

220   How many nights have we slept
    Since passing Niibari
    And Tsukuba?

The Kojiki *records that an old man charged with lighting the fires replied with this song and was rewarded by being made the ruler of the land of Azuma.*

The Nihon Shoki *says that, after all the Emperor's attendants were unable to reply, a lamp-bearer answered with this song and was richly rewarded.*

221   The number of days are, altogether,
    Of nights, nine,
    And of days, ten.

Yamato Takeru returned to the land of Wohari (modern Owari, around Nagoya) and entered the house of his spouse, Miyazu-hime, who prepared a feast for him. When she presented wine to him, he noticed menstrual blood on the skirt of her cloak and made this song.

222   Across the heavenly
      Kagu mountain
    Flies like a sharp sickle
      The long-necked *kubi* bird.

    Your arm slender and delicate
      Like the bird's neck—
    Although I try to sleep
      With it as my pillow,
    Although I intend
      To sleep with you,
    On the skirt
      Of the cloak you are wearing,
    The moon has risen.

In reply to the preceding song, Miyazu-hime sang this song. After the song, they had sexual intercourse, and Yamato Takeru left his sword with Miyazu-hime and went to subdue the god of Mount Ibaki.

223   Oh high shining
       Prince of the Sun,
    Oh my great lord
       Ruling in peace!

    As the years
       Pass by,
    The moons also
       Elapse.

    Truly, no wonder that
       While waiting vainly for you,
    On the cloak
       I am wearing
    The moon should rise.

Emperor Nintoku wished to favor the maiden Kuga-hime, but because of the jealousy of the Empress (Iwa-no-hime), he was unable to summon her; desiring not to cause her to waste her life, he summoned his personal attendants and sang this song to them.

224   Who will foster
           The court maiden,
           Of the deep waters?

In reply to the preceding song, Hayamachi, ancestor of the rulers of the land of Harima, stepped forward and sang this song. Then the Emperor gave the maiden to him, but when he went to visit her the following night, she refused to meet him. Finally she died on her way back to her home.

225   I, Hayamachi of Harima
           Of the great sea-current,
           Though full of awe
           Like a crumbling crag,
           Will foster her.

Songs 226–230 are a sequence of repartee songs between Emperor Nintoku and his Empress (Iwa-no-hime) in 334 A.D. In these songs the Emperor justifies polygamy and the Empress denies its wisdom.

The prose narrative goes that Emperor Nintoku told the Empress that he wished to make the Imperial Princess Yata (see songs 42–43) his concubine (she was his half-sister). The Empress would not consent, and the Emperor sang this song to beseech the Empress.

226 The noble
     Pledges his word—
     He would place two side by side
     Like an extra bowstring,
     To succeed the other should one break.

The song sung by the Empress in reply to the preceding song.

227 Although garments
     May be worn in two layers,
     It is a terrible thing
     That you would lay side by side
     The couches of the night.

Again the Emperor sang this song.

228   The beaches lying side by side
At the point of Naniwa
Of the glittering waves—
It was to lay her side by side
That the maiden existed.

The Empress replied with this song.

229   To wear two layers
Of clothes of summer *mushi* fibers,
Of sun-bleached *mushi* fibers,
And to lodge surrounded by two women,
Is certainly not good.

Again the Emperor sang this song. After this song, the Empress kept silent, refusing to consent and to sing anything in reply.

230   You who walk along the road
Crying alone
On the hill of Hika
Of Asazuma—
It would be better to have a companion.

Songs 231–240 are songs of verbal battle between two love rivals at an utagaki; *songs 231–236 are recorded in the* Kojiki *and attributed to Prince Woke (Emperor Kensō) and his rival Shibi.*

After Prince Woke had been found (see songs 89–90, 263–265) and was about to rule the country, Shibi (literally, "Tuna"), the ancestor of the rulers of Heguri, stood at an utagaki *and took the hand of the maiden whom Prince Woke was about to favor. The maiden's name was Ofuwo (literally, "Great Fish"). Shibi sang this song and demanded an answer in similar form from Prince Woke.*

The song speaks derogatorily of the house of Prince Woke, saying that the corners of its eaves are collapsing.

231 The corners over there
    Of the eaves of your great palace
    Are slumping.

    Reply of Prince Woke to the preceding.

232 It is because
    The carpenter is unskillful
    That the corners are slumping.

    Then Shibi again sang this song.

233 Because the heart
    Of the great lord is slack,
    He does not enter
    The many-layered twig fence
    Of the noble lad.

The Prince sang this song.
Attributed in the Nihon Shoki *to Emperor Muretsu. (See songs 237–*
240.)

234 When I look at the many-layered
     Waves of the ocean shallows,
     By the side of the leisurely swimming
     Shibi
     I see my spouse standing.

Sung by Shibi, who had become more and more enraged.

235 Our great lord
     The prince's twig fence—
     Though it be tied in eight sections,
     Though it be tied clear around,
     It is a twig fence which can be cut,
     It is a twig fence which can be burnt.

Then the Prince sang this song. Thus singing, they fought verbally until dawn and then each went away.

236 Oh fisherman harpooning
     The great fish, the *shibi:*
     If she gets away from you,
     Then, won't you miss her!—
     Oh Shibi harpooning the *shibi!*

After the death of Emperor Ninken in 498 A.D., the Minister of State Heguri-no-Matori wished to usurp the throne and was arrogant to the heir apparent, Prince Waka-sazaki (later Emperor Muretsu). The Prince wished to wed Kage-hime, who had already formed an illicit union with Shibi, son of Matori. The Prince sent a message to Kage-hime that he wished to see her; she replied telling him to come to the public square of Tsuba-ichi (a place in Nara Prefecture). When he approached Kage-hime, suddenly Shibi appeared and stood between them. The Prince sang song 234; then Shibi answered it with this song.

237   Do you mean to ask for admission, oh prince,
Inside the many-layered Chinese fence
Of the noble lad?

Then the Prince sang this song.

238   Standing wearing on my loins
A large sword—
Even though I do not unsheathe it,
Finally in the end
I intend to marry her.

Shibi then sang this in reply.

239   I would make
A many-layered lattice fence
For the great lord,
But since you won't be there,
I do not make it, the lattice fence.

Then the Prince sang this.

240   The many-sectioned twig fence
Of the noble lad—
If the ground rumbles
And an earthquake shakes,
It will break down, that twig fence.

Narrative Songs

Here I have included those songs which seemed to me to be inseparably connected, for one reason or another, with their narratives—songs which are almost meaningless in separation from the narratives in which they are imbedded.

Eight angels once came to bathe in a spring called Manai atop mount Hiji in the land of Tango; an old man and woman, discovering the angels, hid the clothing of one of them, whom they adopted as their daughter. The angel taught them to make a magic wine which cured all illnesses, and by it they became fabulously wealthy. After ten years, the old man and woman drove the unfortunate angel away. Weeping, she sang this song.

241　　　When I look up
　　　　At the vast heavenly plain,
　　　　It is shrouded with mist.
　　　　Unable to tell the way home,
　　　　I know not where to go.

Emperor Sūjin in 88 B.C. sent Ō-biko as a general to pacify the Koshı region. When he had arrived on a certain hill (the Hera hill in Yamashiro, according to the Kojiki), a young woman suddenly appeared and sang this song. When they asked her what she said, she replied: "I am just singing a song." Later it was discovered that this was an omen foretelling a plot against the life of the Emperor.

242　　　Alas, Mimaki-iri-biko!
　　　　Alas, Mimaki-iri-biko,
　　　　You do not know
　　　　　　That they are plotting against your life,
　　　　Going around
　　　　　　From the back door,
　　　　Going around
　　　　　　From the front door,
　　　　Looking in at you—
　　　Alas, Mimaki-iri-biko!

During the reign of Emperor Sūjin, a princess called Yamato-toto-hi-momo-so-hime became the wife of the god Ō-mono-nushi, who visited her only at night and never appeared during the day. When she found that his true form was that of a little snake, she was filled with remorse for having shamed him and died. When her tomb was being constructed, men worked on it during the day, and gods worked on it at night. Rocks were passed by laborers from hand to hand from Mt. Ōsaka to the grave, and a contemporary made this song.

243   These many rocks
            Which are one after another
            Going up Mount Ōsaka—
            If they are passed thus from hand to hand,
            Will they ever be able to cross the mountain?

Local legend has it that during the reign of Emperor Suinin (traditionally 29 B.C.–70 A.D.), white swans would fly down every day to the village of Shiro-tori (literally, "White Bird") in Kashima County in the land of Hitachi. The swans would turn into maidens and would pile up stones in order to build a pond. But they were unable to complete the bank of the pond, and, while singing this song, they ascended into the skies, never to return again. For this reason, the village is called Shiro-tori.

244   Even though we were
            To build a bank with feathers
            Of white swans,
            Alas, there would be no time to wash . . .

According to the Kojiki, *Yamato Takeru made friends with his foe, Izumo Takeru, and went to bathe with him in the river. Having first exchanged swords and replaced his enemy's sword with a wooden sword, he challenged him to a duel and killed him, singing this song to taunt him.*

In the Nihon Shoki, *this song was sung by contemporaries about Ii-iri-ne, who had been killed by his elder brother Izumo Furune when he sent the divine treasures of the shrine of Izumo to Emperor Sūjin in the absence of the elder brother.*

The Kojiki *makes the song a taunting song sung about a dead enemy, while the* Nihon Shoki *makes it a song by contemporaries expressing sympathy with the younger brother. In both cases, the victims were killed by treachery after their swords had been surreptitiously changed for wooden swords.*

245 The sword
    Worn by Izumo Takeru
    (Of the rising clouds)
    Has many vines wrapped around it,
    But has no blade inside,
    Alas!

After the death of Emperor Ōjin (in 310 A.D.), Prince Ō-sazaki (later Emperor Nintoku), in obedience to the late Emperor's will, ceded his right to the throne to his younger brother, Prince Uji. Then Prince Ō-yama-mori, wishing to usurp the throne himself, attempted to kill Prince Uji, but was the victim of the latter's plot when his boat was overturned and he was plunged into the Uji River. He sang this song while floating down the river to his death.

246 At the crossing
    Of the river Uji
    Of the raging billows,
    Someone quick at the rudder—
    Oh come to my aid!

During the reign of Emperor Nintoku (313–399 A.D.), a giant camphor tree was cut down and made into a marvelously fast boat, called Hayatori ("Fast Bird"). The boat used to bring, morning and evening, water from the spring of Komate at Akashi for the Emperor's meals at the palace of Naniwa. This is a song about the boat when one day it did not arrive in time with the water for the Emperor's meal.

247 Only if it flies
    Toward the imperial store-house
    Of Sumi-no-e
    Is it to be called "Fast Bird"—
    How can it be called "Fast Bird"?

According to the Kojiki, *during the reign of Emperor Nintoku, a giant tree was cut down and made into a boat, which was very fast and was named Karano. It was used to carry water for the Emperor's table from the island of Awaji. Finally the boat became useless and was burnt for salt; the remaining timber that was not burnt was made into a* koto, *the sound of which re-echoed for seven leagues. Therefore this song was sung.*

In the Nihon Shoki *account, the government ship sent as tribute by the land of Izu became rotten and unfit for use; it was burnt for salt, but some of the wood left over was presented to Emperor Ōjin, who had it made into a* koto, *which resounded far off. Then the Emperor made this song.*

248 The ship Karano
     Was burnt for salt,
    And the remaining wood
     Was made into a *koto*:
    When its strings were plucked,
    It was like the plants
    Growing on the underwater rocks
    In the Yura channel
    Which sway languidly—
    Saya saya.

Songs 249–251 are connected with the story of Prince Hayabusa-wake and Princess Medori.

Emperor Nintoku wished to take his half-sister Princess Medori as his concubine, and employed his younger brother Prince Hayabusa-wake as go-between. But instead Hayabusa-wake and Medori secretly became man and wife, and Hayabusa-wake did not report back to the Emperor. The Emperor went to Princess Medori's chamber and, seeing that she was weaving on her loom, sang this song.

249   For whom is intended
The garment being woven
By my lady
Medori?

The song of Princess Medori in reply to the preceding song.

250   It is cloth for a coat
For the high-flying falcon,
Hayabusa-wake!

According to the Kojiki, *when Prince Hayabusa-wake came to visit Princess Medori, she sang this song. The Emperor, hearing it, raised troops and set out to kill them.*

251   The lark
Flies high in the sky.
Oh high-flying falcon,
Hayabusa-wake,
Seize the wagtail!

A plot was made on the life of Emperor Richū (in 399 A.D.), and Achi-no-atae, ancestor of the immigrant family Yamato-no-Aya-no-atae, spirited the Emperor out of the burning palace and, putting him on horseback, led him away towards Yamato. When they arrived at the Plain of Tajihi, the Emperor awoke and asked "Where are we?" Achi-no-atae told of the plot and said that they were bound for Yamato. Then the Emperor sang this song.

252   If I had known that I would sleep
                On the plain of Tajihi,
                I would have brought
                A rush mat,
                If I had known that I would sleep.

When they arrived at the hill of Hanifu, the Emperor looked back towards the palace of Naniwa, which was still burning, and sang this song.

253   On Hanifu hill
                When I stood and looked,
                The sun's rays were shimmering
                Around the group of houses—
                Where my wife's house stood.

As they entered the road to Ōsaka pass, they met a maiden who warned them that there were many armed men in the mountains and urged them to take the Tagima road. Thereupon, the Emperor sang this song.

254   On Ōsaka pass
                I met a maiden.
                On asking the way of her,
                She said not to go straight ahead,
                But to take the Tagima road.

Because of Prince Ki-nashi-no-Karu's incestuous relations with his sister, popular favor shifted to Prince Anaho (later Emperor Ankō). Prince Anaho pursued Prince Karu to the house of Ōmae-Womae-no-sukune and surrounded the house with troops. When Prince Anaho reached the gate, it was raining, and he sang this song.

255 Come thus under the shelter
     Of the gate
     Of Ōmae-
     Womae-sukune
     And wait for the rain to cease.

(Following the previous song.) In the Kojiki, *this is the song sung by Ōmae-Womae-no-sukune, as he (or they) came out, lifting up his hands, hitting his thighs, and dancing and singing.*

256 Because the little bell
     On the garter of the noble courtier
     Fell off,
     The courtiers are all astir.
     Commoners also, take care!

In 456 A.D., Prince Mayowa, who had murdered Emperor Ankō, fled with Imperial Prince Sakaahi-no-Kuro-hiko to the house of Tsubura-no-ōmi. When Tsubura refused to surrender the princes to Emperor Yūryaku, the Emperor surrounded the house with an army. Tsubura came out into the yard and asked for his garters. His wife brought them and sang this song in great sorrow and anguish. Later the Emperor burnt the house down, and everyone perished in the flames.

257   The noble lord,
            Wearing seven pairs
            Of trousers of *tae* cloth,
            Stands in the yard
            And adjusts his garters.

When Emperor Yūryaku was hunting in 460 A.D., a horse-fly bit his arm. Immediately a dragonfly appeared and devoured the horse-fly. Thereupon the Emperor composed this song.

258   News that game were lying
On the mountain peak Womura
Of Yoshino
Was reported by someone
To the Emperor.

As our great lord
Awaited the game,
Seated upon his dais,
On his arm,
Clad in a sleeve
Of white *tae* cloth,
Landed a horse-fly.
This horse-fly
Was quickly devoured
By a dragon-fly.

Thus, in order to perpetuate
The memory of this event,
Is the sky-full
Land of Yamato called
The Dragon-fly Island.

According to the Kojiki, *once when Emperor Yūryaku was hunting on Mount Kazuraki, he shot a huge wild boar, which charged at him. The Emperor, fearing the snorting of the animal, climbed up into a black alder tree, where he sang this song.*

In the Nihon Shoki, *when the boar charged, the Emperor's huntsmen and attendant all climbed up into trees, and the Emperor himself killed the beast. As he was about to kill the attendant for his cowardice, the attendant sang this song. The Empress, hearing this song, prevailed upon the Emperor to spare the attendant's life.*

259   Fearing the snorting
            Of the beast,
            The wounded beast
            Shot by our great lord,
            I ran away and climbed
            Up a branch of the black alder tree
            On the hill!

In 469 A.D., *Emperor Yūryaku fined Hatane-no-mikoto eight horses and eight swords for his crime of seducing the* uneme *(court lady) Koshima-ko from Yama-no-be. After paying the fine, he sang this song, which was reported to the Emperor, who then imposed further punishments.*

260   I do not regret in the least
            To part with eight horses
            Of which anyone would be proud,
            For the sake of Koshima-ko
            Of Yama-no-be.

The carpenter Inabe-no-Mane used to plane timber with an axe, using a stone as a base, and never injuring his axe. Emperor Yūryaku visited the place and asked him if he ever made a mistake and struck the stone. He replied in the negative. Then the Emperor assembled the uneme *(court ladies) and had them strip and wrestle in the open with only their panties on. When Mane looked up and unawares ruined his axe, the Emperor was angry and handed him over to be executed. One of his fellow-carpenters sang this song lamenting for him.*

The ink-string is a thread passed through India ink and used to mark straight lines on lumber; it is used by Japanese carpenters instead of pencils. Here it is a metaphor for the carpenter.

261   Oh the ink-string
            Applied by the unfortunate
            Carpenter Inabe!

            Without him,
            Who will be able to apply it?
            Alas, poor ink-string!

The Emperor, hearing the preceding song, regretted his action and sent a messenger of pardon on a black pony from the land of Kai to stay the execution. Again, this song was sung.

262   The jet-black
            Pony from Kai—
            If it had been saddled,
            His life would have been lost—
            Oh, black pony from Kai!

This is the song given in the Kojiki *by which Prince Woke (Emperor Kensō) announced his identity (compare with the* Nihon Shoki *account attached to songs 89–90 and the* Harima Fudoki *account in songs 264–265).*

Wodate, the governor of the land of Harima, attended a celebration in honor of the dedication of a new house by an inhabitant called Shijimu. When each person danced in turn at the feast, the two young brothers who tended the fire were also asked to dance. The assemblage laughed at them when they politely yielded to each other; then finally the elder brother danced first, followed by the younger brother, who chanted these words when about to dance. After hearing these words, Wodate realized these boys were the long-lost princes, sons of Prince Oshiha, and brought them back to the palace.

263   My beloved
Warrior lad
Is wearing
A sword, on the hilt of which
Is daubed red clay,
On the cord of which
Is attached a red banner.

When the red banner is erected
It conceals
The ridges of the mountains.

The mountain bamboo,
When cut down
And spread out in rows;
An eight-stringed *koto*,
When played in perfect tune—

Like this he ruled the land,
The son of the Emperor
Izaho-wake,
Ichi-no-be-no-
Oshi-ha-no-miko—
His offspring are we!

According to the account in the Harima Fudoki, *Princes Oke and Woke were employed in the household of Itomi, chief of the village of Shijimi. At a feast for a new home celebrated by Itomi, the younger brother, Prince Woke, sang this and the following song.*

264   As if hoeing a field
             With a hoe
             Made of iron
             From Kibi—
             Clap your hands, my lads:
             I am about to dance.

After the preceding song, Prince Woke sang this song. Hearing it, everyone was afraid and ran out. Word of this incident reached Wodate, who had been sent to govern the mountains (yama-be) of the land of Harima. He then arranged the restoration of the princes to their rightful position.

265   Afumi
             Is a land of gathered waters.
             Yamato is surrounded by
             Green partitions of mountains.
             In green-partitioned
             Yamato dwelt
             The Emperor
             Ichi-no-be,
             Whose offspring
             Are we!

After Prince Woke had ascended the throne as Emperor Kensō, he began to search for the bones of his murdered father. An old woman, Okime, knew the place where they were buried, and informed the Emperor. In gratitude to her, the Emperor caused her to dwell near the palace and suspended a large bell at the door of the palace, which he rang whenever he wished to summon her. He therefore made this song.

In the Nihon Shoki, *the Emperor stretched out a rope to support the old woman as she walked; at the end of the rope he attached a bell for her to ring to announce her approach. The Emperor, hearing this bell, made this song.*

266   Across the reed-plains,
           Across the valleys
           Resounding,
           Reverberates the bell.
           Okime is sure to come.

In 486 A.D., the old woman Okime asked leave to return to her native place, since she was now decrepit with old age. The Emperor sang this song at parting from her.

267   Oh Okime,
           Okime of Afumi,
           From tomorrow,
           Hidden behind the mountains.
           You will no longer be seen!

After Kena-no-omi was relieved of his post as resident in Mimana (Imna, the Japanese colony in Korea), Mezura-ko was sent to replace him in 530 A.D. This is a song made by the Japanese officials there on the occasion of Mezura-ko's arrival.

268   Ah what is to be said
       Of the land of Kara?
       Mezura-ko has come.

       Across the far-away
       Sea-crossing of Iki,
       Mezura-ko has come.

In 562 A.D., Silla defeated the Japanese colony Mimana and the Japanese army. Among those taken prisoner by the Silla army was Tsuki-no-Kishi-Ikina, a Korean from Paekche. When he refused to submit, he was put to death. His wife, Ōbako, who was taken captive at the same time, in her grief made this song.

269   Standing atop the fortress
       In the land of Kara,
       Ōbako
       Waves her scarf
       Towards Yamato.

In response to the preceding song, someone made this song.

270   Standing atop the fortress
       In the land of Kara,
       Ōbako is seen
       To wave her scarf
       Towards Naniwa.

When Prince Shōtoku in 613 A.D. was traveling to Kata-woka, he came upon a starving man lying by the road. He gave him food and drink and clothed him with his own clothing, then made this song. Later it was learned that the starving man had died, but on inspecting his tomb, it was discovered that the corpse had miraculously disappeared.

271   Alas, poor traveler
Lying,
Starved for food
On Kata-woka mountain
Of the shining steps!

Were you born
Without parents?
Have you no lord?

Alas, poor traveler,
Lying,
Starved for food!

Prince Shōtoku in 619 received an Imperial command to travel around the Home Provinces and inspect the Buddhist temples built by the local governors. When he arrived east of Shii-zaka, he looked towards his palace and sang this song to himself.

272   My heart rushes in
Among the flames
Of the burning fire
On the tiles of the palace
Of Ikaruga.

During the struggle for the throne after the death of Empress Suiko, Soga-no-Emishi, the prime minister, murdered Sakaibe-no-omi and his second son Aya. But the eldest son Ketsu escaped and, after hiding in a nunnery, was denounced by one of the nuns and escaped to Mt. Unebi, where, finally unable to elude his pursuers any longer, he killed himself. A contemporary sang this song. This was in 628 A.D.

273   Although the trees
      Grow sparsely on Mount Unebi,
      The youth Ketsu
      Must have hidden there
      Relying on them for protection.

During the year 642 A.D., Soga-no-Emishi erected a temple for his ancestors at Takamiya in Kazuraki and had performed an eight-row dance—an assumption of imperial rank. He sang this song.

274   In order to cross
      The wide ford at Oshi
      In Yamato,
      I tie up my garters
      And gird my loins.

Miscellaneous Songs

Besides the songs for which I could find no place elsewhere, I have included here in a body, the songs from the *Kakyō Hyōshiki* (songs 289–313).

After the death of Emperor Jimmu (traditionally in 585 B.C.), the elder half-brother of the Emperor married the Empress, Princess Isukeyori, and plotted to murder the three sons of the Emperor. The Empress sang this and the following song to warn her three sons of the impending danger.

275   Clouds are rising
       From the Sai river;
       On Unebi mountain
       The leaves of the trees are rustling;
       Soon the wind will begin to blow.

276   On Unebi mountain,
       During the day the clouds shift restlessly;
       Now it is night,
       And as if to warn that the wind is about to blow,
       The leaves of the trees are rustling.

After Kuro-hime had departed for her homeland, Emperor Nintoku yearned for her and, deceiving the Empress Iwa-no-hime by telling her that he was going to the island of Awaji, set out to visit Kuro-hime in her home at Kibi. When he was in Awaji on the way, he looked out far into the distance and sang this song.

277   Setting out
      From the point of Naniwa
      Of the glittering waves,
      I survey my country
      And behold
      The island of Awa,
      The island of Onogoro,
      The island of Ajimasa,
      And of Saketsu-shima.

While the Empress Iwa-no-hime was traveling in the land of Ki, the Emperor Nintoku brought Princess Yata into the palace. When the Empress arrived back at Naniwa, she heard this news and was extremely angry, refusing to land. The Emperor, unaware of the Empress's anger, went in person to meet her ship and sang this song.

278   Oh men of Naniwa,
        Catch the boat with the bell!
        Plunging up to your waists in the water,
        Catch that boat,
        Catch that august boat!

The Empress Iwa-no-hime, hearing that Emperor Nintoku had wedded Princess Yata in her absence, refused to return to the palace, but went up the river towards Yamashiro (singing here song 97). From Yamashiro she went towards Nara Mountain, where she sang this song looking out at the Kazuraki region.

279   As I ascend,
          As I ascend to the palace,
      Up the Yamashiro river,
          Of many mountain peaks,
      I pass by Nara
          Of the blue clay,
      I pass by Yamato
          Of the little shields;
      The country which I wish to see
      Is Takamiya in Kazuraki,
      Where my home is.

When the Empress went up towards Yamashiro, the Emperor sent an attendant called Toriyama to bring the Empress back, singing this song.

280   To Yamashiro
      Catch up with her, Toriyama,
      Catch up, catch up with her!
      With my beloved wife
      Catch up and meet her!

Emperor Nintoku sent Kuchi-ko-no-omi (in one version, Kuchi-mochi-no-omi) to take a message to Empress Iwa-no-hime, who was staying at the house of the Korean Nurinomi in Tsutsuki in Yamashiro. The Empress refused to listen to the message, and the messenger remained outside during a storm. The messenger's younger sister, who happened to be attending the Empress, grieved at her brother's piteous plight and sang this song. Nevertheless, the Empress refused to return.

281   I am moved to tears
      At the sight of my brother,
      Who is speaking his message
      In the palace of Tsutsuki
      Of Yamashiro.

Finally the Emperor himself went up the river towards Yamashiro to fetch the Empress. At this time, a mulberry branch came floating down the stream. Seeing it, the Emperor made this song.

282   The princess
                Iwa-no-hime
                Does not speak generously
                Of the mulberry branch.

                Drifting hither and thither
                Along the river bends,
                Which it ought not approach,
                Comes the mulberry branch.

When Emperor Nintoku arrived at the house of Nurinomi, where the Empress Iwa-no-hime was staying, he stood at the door and sang this song.

283   The maiden of Yamashiro
                    Of many mountain peaks
                With a wooden-handled hoe
                    Digs up white *daikon* radishes
                With a noisy sound—
                    Since you have spoken so noisily,
                Like luxuriantly flourishing trees
                    Viewed from afar,
                Many of us have come in.

A poem written on an ivory shaku *(ceremonial scepter) preserved at Gangoji Temple.*

284   Ah my beloved lord
            Whose beauty I adore—
            With this in your hand,
            May you frequent the Court—
            For countless ages!

A poem found written on the back of a document (dated 749 A.D.) in the Shōsō-in in Nara, evidently written by a weary scribe. This is the oldest piece of Japanese verse of which we possess the original written document.

285   The red cockscomb flowers
            By my house,
            When I look at them now—
            They can no longer
            Be used for dyes.

In 717 A.D., Abe-no-Nakamaro was sent as a student to T'ang China. Although he tried to return to Japan, he was not able to make the return journey and finally died in service of the T'ang Court at the age of 70, in the year 770 A.D. This was a song of nostalgia composed by him in China.

286   As I look far out
            Across the plain of heaven—
            Ah, it is the same moon
            Which appeared above Mount Mikasa
            In my native Kasuga.

Evidently a song praising a dandy.

287   Wearing hanging from your waist
               A sword decorated
               With ornaments of silver—
               Through the capital of Nara
               Who is this lad strolling?
               Who is this lad strolling?

*Evidently a folk song dating from the period when the capital was at Kuni
(714–744 A.D.).*

288   The Sawada river
               Is shallow enough
               To wet one's sleeves—
               But the courtiers of Kuni
               Span a high bridge over it.

The following 25 songs are taken from the Kakyō Hyōshiki *and tend to be literary poems in the* Manyō *style rather than ancient songs.*

This song is an elegy by Princess Ōku (661–701 A.D.), yearning for her brother Prince Ōtsu, who was executed in 686 A.D. The Princess came to the capital from the Grand Shrine of Ise, where she was high priestess, on the 16th of the 11th month, only to find that her brother had already been executed on the 3rd of the 10th month.

289   Now that you,
         Whom I longed to see,
         Are no longer,
         Ah, to what point have I come—
         Tiring the horses in vain?

This is a song, evidently of romantic invitation, bestowed by Emperor Suinin (reigned traditionally 29 B.C.–70 A.D.) upon a maiden called Yasaka-iri-hime (mentioned in the Nihon Shoki *as the consort of Emperor Keikō, the son of Emperor Suinin).*

290   There is no shade on the hill
         Where the great lord resides;
         This pear tree,
         When planted and caused to grow,
         Will be good for shade.

The reply of Yasaka-iri-hime to the preceding song.

291   This pear tree,
         If planted and caused to grow,
         Will be overwhelmed with awe.

Identified by the Kakyō Hyōshiki *as a poem by Princess Tajima (died 708 A.D.) in reply to Prince Hozumi (died 715 A.D.).*

According to the Manyōshū, *Prince Hozumi and Princess Tajima had clandestine relations, even though they were half-brother and -sister.*

292   Why should my mind
                Stir now?—
                Now that my submissive
                Heart has yielded
                To you, my lord?

Attributed to Prince Nagata (died 737 A.D.) yearning for a certain woman.

293   I have not met my beloved
                For such a long time
                As conspicuous as the crystal dew
                Causing the foliage to change color
                On the autumn mountains.

Love song of Prince Shio-yaki (flourished 724–758 A.D.)

294   It is as the seaweed
                By the shore, hidden under water
                When the tides are high—
                The days of seeing her are few,
                And the nights of longing are many.

Song by Tagima-no-tayu (dates unknown) when accompanying the Imperial progress (year unknown) to Ise and yearning to return home.

295   The flowerless gulfweed
Of the bay of Hikitsu
Of the drawn *azusa* bow—
Until even it blossoms into flowers—
So long have I not seen my beloved!

Love song by Ōtomo-no-Shimeya-no-wakugo (not identified).

296   The white flowers
Of the wild strawberries
Blooming right by the road—
Open for all to see,
Shall I yearn?

Recorded as by Fujiwara-no-Kamatari (died 669 A.D.).

297   The cord of my beloved,
When undone, I tie up again
And stand up: Tatsuta mountain—
As far as one can see, the foliage
Of the autumn fields has changed color.

Recorded as the work of Emperor Temmu (673–686 A.D.).

298

The good person who,
Looking well at Mi-yoshino,
Said that it was good—
That good person
Had looked well at Yoshino.

Song by Kagami-no-ōkimi, a princess of the Ōmi period, who died in 683 A.D., according to the Nihon Shoki.

299

The young willow buds
Have already turned into green thread-like branches:
During all this time we have not met—
Regretfully I braid
Willow branches into my hair.

Song by Ōmiwa-no-Takechi-Maro (died 706 A.D.).

300

The mountains shrouded
In trailing white clouds
Are a sight of which I never tire.

If only I were a crane,
I could go flying over them in the morning
And come back in the evening!

Presented by Kaki-no-moto-no-Hitomaro to Prince Naga (died 715 A.D.).

301   Catching in a net
        The moon moving across
        The far-flung skies,
        Our great lord
        Has made it into his silken awning.

Song by Kaki-no-moto-no-Hitomaro.

302   The river Hatsuse
            Of the hidden country
        So clear that even the clouds in the sky
            Are reflected in it—
        Is it because it has no sheltering coves?
            No boats approach it;
        Is it because it has no beaches?
            The fishermen do not fish there.

        Oh well if there
            Be no sheltering coves!
        Oh well if there
            Be no beaches!
        Come rowing in nevertheless,
            Pure as the waves of the offing,
            You boats of the fishermen!

Composed by Tsuno-no-Sami at a beach in Kishū (present Wakayama Prefecture).

303   The offerings hung
   On the branches of the pine trees
   By the billowy beach
   How many ages
   Have gone by?

Composed by Tsuno-no-Sami in praise of a beautiful woman.

304   The name of my beloved
   Will be handed down for a thousand ages—
   Until the branches
   Of the pines of Hime island
   Are covered with moss.

Presented by Fujiwara-no-Maro (died 737 A.D.) to Imperial Prince Niitabe (died 735 A.D.).

305   The pearls hidden
   Deep under the sea—
   I am not one to give
   My whole heart to profound devotion
   For someone's sake!

A riddle song by Fujiwara-no-Hamanari.

306   The house of a mouse—
Grinding rice—
Cutting a tree
And kindling it—
Four—is it this?

Poem by Wo-hatsuse-no-Ugai (not identified) on Tama-tsu-shima island.

307   After I have returned to Yamato,
I shall long for it—
The sea-strait between the islands
Of the sea of Sahika
In the land of Ki.

Nonsense song by Kume-no-Hirotari.

308   Mount Kasuga—
A boat rowing over the peak
Of Yakushi temple.
The island of Awaji,
The blade of a plough.

Song by the priest Dōgō (not identified).

309   Like a rope
Climbing up on
A banner-pole—
Like a banner-pole
Climbing up . . .

Song by Eguri-no-Toyoshima (not identified).

310
The cocks are crowing
To announce the dawn;
And the bells
Of the temples are resounding.
Dawn has come, this night is over.

Anonymous.

311
Through the ravines
Of fairest Mount Nara,
This which is trailing
Like pure white *tae* cloth
Is the spring mist.

Anonymous.

312
At the wind's blowing,
The clouds rise like silken awnings
On Mount Tatsuta,
Which is like a morning-glory
Radiantly blooming.

Anonymous.

313
The autumn bush-clover flowers
Have bloomed and must now be falling—
In sadness at the sound
Of the deer crying
In the plain of Kasuga.

Notes

1 (*Nihon Shoki* 3; *Z* 4)

See no. 95.

Identified by the musical name *Hina-buri* (also applied to nos. 95 and 271), which name may be derived from the word *hina* (meaning "country") in the second line of the song.

The song is usually interpreted as a song of invitation addressed either to women or to a deity. The *Kagura* songs also contain an example of a song of romantic invitation being used to summon a deity.

2 (*Kojiki* 85; *Z* 232)

See no. 19. The song does not fit the circumstances given in the narrative and is obviously a song of romantic invitation.

This song, as well as nos. 32 and 50, is identified by the musical name *Amada-buri*; each of them begins with the words *ama-damu* or *ama-tobu* (both meaning "sky-flying"), whence was derived the musical appellation.

Karu is a place in Nara Prefecture. The words "sky-flying" constitute a *makura-kotoba* (a fixed epithet) modifying the proper noun Karu, which is similar in sound to the noun *kari*, or wild goose. The *makura-kotoba* does not apply to the maidens, but merely to the place name with which they are identified.

3 (*Nihon Shoki* 124; *Z* 89)

Yae-ko is the name of a girl; and Tamade is a common place name found in various regions.

4 (*Kojiki* 2; *Z* 165)

There is a confusion of person in this song, much commented upon by literary historians. The first paragraph is in the third person; then the second paragraph changes into the first person.

The musical name for this song and the songs following it is *Kamu-gatari* ("God-narrative").

The final lines are a formula identifying the carrier as belonging to an ancient clan, the Amabe, who were employed as reciters or bards in the Court. The meaning of the words *ishitafu ya* is not known; they are evidently a *makura-kotoba* modifying the following line.

5 (*Kojiki* 3; *Z* 166)

The *Kojiki* narrative says that Princess Nunakawa, without opening the doors, sang this song from inside the house.

6 (*Kojiki* 4; *Z* 167)

The second song of reply of Princess Nunakawa.

After the song, the *Kojiki* narrative relates that they were not united that night, but were united the following night.

The final formula is here abbreviated to three lines, as also in other songs.

7 (*Kojiki* 5; *Z* 168)

Another *Kojiki* song connected with the god Ya-chi-hoko. The narrative follows immediately after the preceding song.

The references to the various types of clothes present certain problems in interpretation. One likes to think of this and other songs in this series as having been acted out as primitive dramas.

As yet there is no satisfactory explanation of why clothes dyed with the juice of pounded *atane* plants should be more acceptable than the black or blue clothes to a husband leaving his wife. *Atane* juice is sometimes explained as being a brilliant red dye, but this explanation is also doubtful.

8 (*Kojiki* 6; *Z* 169)
Songs 4–8 are all identified by the musical name *Kamu-gatari* and are believed to have been part of the traditions carried by the clan of Amabe.

9 (*Nihon Shoki* 96; *Z* 269)
This song is recorded in the *Nihon Shoki* in connection with an entirely different personage, but is obviously a variant of song 4.
The *Manyōshū* also contains another variant of the same song (no. 3310). Songs of this type were evidently widely distributed.
Hi: modern Japanese *hinoki*, Japanese cypress.

10 (*Nihon Shoki* 4; *Z* 170)

11 (*Kojiki* 62; *Nihon Shoki* 58; *Z* 209)
The *Kojiki* records this song after song 41. Other songs connected with the same narrative are given in the Miscellaneous section (songs 279–283).
Designated by the musical name *Shitsu-uta no utai-kaeshi*.
The first four verses are introductory.
Modern commentators almost unanimously agree in indicating the folk song qualities of this song.

12 (*Kojiki* 8; *Z* 171)

13 (*Nihon Shoki* 6; *Z* 172)
The version given in the *Nihon Shoki* in connection with the same narrative.
Identified with the musical name *Age-uta*.

14 (*Kojiki* 9; *Nihon Shoki* 5; *Kakyō Hyōshiki*; *Z* 173)
The *Nihon Shoki* identifies this song, like song 13, with the musical name *Age-uta*.

15 (*Owari no kuni Atsuta Jingū Engi*; *Z* 182)
The songs are identified with the musical name *Kuni-buri-uta*, a name usually applied to local folk songs.

16 (*Owari no kuni Atsuta Jingū Engi*; *Z* 183)

17 (*Nihon Shoki* 40; *Z* 191)
Awaji is the present island of Awaji; Azuki is the present Shōdo Island: both islands in the Inland Sea.

18 (*Nihon Shoki* 68; *Z* 225)

19 (*Kojiki* 87; *Nihon Shoki* 70; *Z* 234)
The musical name is *Hina-buri no kata-oroshi*; the song is extremely similar in metrical form and diction to song 42.
"Great lord" probably refers to the speaker.
Line 3 is evidently a *makura-kotoba* modifying the word for "return."

20 (*Kojiki* 89; *Z* 236)
The same song appears twice in the *Manyōshū*. One version (no. 90) is identical with the *Kojiki* version; but the other (no. 85) differs slightly in wording. On the left I have given the *Kojiki* text, and on the right the text of *Manyōshū* 85:

Kimi ga yuki	Kimi ga yuki
Ke-nagaku narinu	Ke-nagaku narinu
Yama-tazu no	Yama tazune
Mukae wo yukamu	Mukae ka yukamu
Matsu ni wa mataji	Machi ni ka matamu

In the third line, the *Manyōshū* version has *yama tazune* ("seeking across the mountains") instead of *yama tazu no* ("like the *yama-tazu* tree"); here, as in other cases, one small phonetic change results in a wide divergence in meaning. The meaning of the above-quoted *Manyō* version is as follows:

> Since you have set out,
> Many days have passed.
> Seeking across the mountains,
> Shall I go in search of you,
> Or shall I wait?

The *yama-tazu* tree is identified as the *Sambucus Sieboldiana* and is used as a *makura-kotoba* for the word *mukae*, "to go after."

The *Manyōshū* 85 version is attributed to the Empress Iwa-no-hime as a song of yearning for Emperor Nintoku.

21 (*Kojiki* 90; *Z* 237)

Both 21 and 22, as well as 108, are identified by the musical name *Yomi-uta*.

This song is extremely difficult of interpretation. The first six verses, containing mention of banners, may refer to funeral ceremonies.

Hatsuse is present Hase in Nara prefecture.

Tsuki and *azusa* are both trees providing the wood for bows.

22 (*Kojiki* 91; *Z* 238)

Like songs 21 and 108, identified as a *Yomi-uta*.

The *Manyōshū* contains a variant of the same song (no. 3263).

The imagery seems to be that of a funeral, and it is quite possible that it was an elegy rather than a love song.

23 (*Tango Fudoki*; *Z* 251)

This legend appears also in the *Manyōshū* (nos. 1740 and 1741) and in the *Nihon Shoki*, which records it as happening in the year 478 A.D.

Song 23 is the song sung by the boy of Urashima while weeping over his misfortune.

24 (*Tango Fudoki*; *Z* 252)

A reply sent by the princess. A variant of song 30.

25 (*Tango Fudoki*; *Z* 253)

Another song sung by the boy, unable to conquer his yearning. *Toko-yo*—the Eternal World—is the ancient Japanese Paradise of eternal life and beatitude far across the ocean.

26 (*Tango Fudoki*; *Z* 254)

A song by someone later to comment on the Urashima legend.

27 (*Nihon Ryōiki*; *Z* 273)

Appears also in the *Manyōshū* (nos. 3085, 2394) and was evidently widely distributed.

28 (*Kojiki* 25; *Z* 181)
   Spoke my name: or, inquired for my safety.

29 (*Kojiki* 53; *Z* 192)
   Masazuko is evidently a name applied to Kuro-hime.

30 (*Kojiki* 56; *Z* 195)
   A variant of song 24.

31 (*Kojiki* 57; *Z* 196)
   The stealthy return of the Emperor towards Yamato is compared to the flowing of an underground brook.

32 (*Kojiki* 86; *Z* 233)
   See song 19.
   Identified by the musical name *Amada-buri* (see also songs 2 and 50).

33 (*Kojiki* 88; *Z* 235)
   Clearly ought to be considered apart from the accompanying narrative. No doubt a song of a woman in a fishing village who wishes to detain her lover. Similar verse abounds in the *Manyōshū*; see, for instance, no. 3399.
   The location of Ahine is not identified. Ahine may also mean "sleep together," and no doubt this double meaning was intentional.

34 (*Kojiki* 20; *Z* 178)
   In the *Kojiki*, narrative follows song 216.

35 (*Kojiki* 43; *Z* 186)
   In this song, which is a typical example of antique poetic expression, the speaker puts himself in the place of a crab; evidently crab meat figured in the feast, thus providing the excuse for this love song.
   Tsunuga is present-day Tsuruga in Fukui Prefecture.
   Sasanami is a place on the southern shore of Lake Biwa, near Ōtsu City.
   Kohata is a place name in present Uji City.
   Both Wani and Ichi-i are places in Nara Prefecture.

36 (*Kojiki* 44; *Nihon Shoki* 35; *Z* 187)
   The versions of the *Kojiki* and *Nihon Shoki* vary slightly; I have chosen the *Kojiki* version here.
   Hiru is a wild plant somewhat like an onion. Wild rocambole; *Allium nipponicum.*
   Tachibana—a type of tangerine tree bearing small fruits. *Citrus aurantium var. tachibana Makino.*
   "Three chestnut," Japanese *mitsu-guri*, is a *makura-kotoba* modifying the word *naka*, "middle, center." Chestnuts are found three in a pod.

37 (*Kojiki* 45; *Nihon Shoki* 36; *Z* 188)
   The *Nihon Shoki*, however, makes it a song of reply by Prince Ō-sazaki.
   The versions of the *Kojiki* and *Nihon Shoki* differ to a certain degree; here I have given the *Kojiki* version.
   Evidently it is a song expressing the self-derision of the Emperor at not having been aware of his son's liking for the maiden.
   Nunaha is a kind of edible water plant called *junsai* in modern Japanese; *Brasenia Schreberi Gmel.*

38 (*Kojiki* 46; *Nihon Shoki* 37; *Z* 189)

39 (*Kojiki* 47; *Nihon Shoki* 38; *Z* 190)

40 (*Kojiki* 55; *Z* 194)

41 (*Kojiki* 61; *Z* 208)
See songs 11, 279–283.
The first six lines are a long introductory portion leading up to the main subject in the last two lines. The song seems to have little connection with the narrative.
Designated by the musical name *Shitsu-uta no utai-kaeshi*.
Mimoro was originally a common noun meaning a place where a deity is enshrined, but later came to be a proper noun usually applied to Mount Miwa, the sacred mountain in Nara prefecture.

42 (*Kojiki* 65; *Z* 213)
Similar in metrical form to song 19.

43 (*Kojiki* 66; *Z* 214)
The song is in the *sedōka* form, consisting of six verses of 5-7-7-5-7-7 syllables each.

44 (*Nihon Shoki* 65; *Z* 222)
A variant version appears in the *Kokinshū*.

45 (*Nihon Shoki* 66; *Z* 223)
Evidently the meaning is: "It has been only one night that I untied my garments and slept with you to the full." The following interpretation is also possible: "The cord which you tied on my garments as a token of our troth—I have untied it and slept with another only one night." The *Manyōshū* contains numerous references to cords tied as tokens of love.

46 (*Nihon Shoki* 67; *Z* 224)

47 (*Kojiki* 76; *Nihon Shoki* 69; *Kinkafu*; *Z* 226)
The *Kinkafu* also carries an account attributing the song to Emperor Ingyō who sang it when he slept with Princess So-tōshi.
I have given the version of the *Kojiki*.
The *Kojiki* and *Kinkafu* identify the song with the musical name *Shiragi-uta* (or *Shirage-uta*).
There is a resemblance between the metrical form of this song and that of ancient Korean songs of the Silla period. It has been suggested that this song was performed to the accompaniment of Korean music, and that the name *Shiragi-uta* means "Korean song"—Shiragi being the Japanese pronunciation of the word Silla.

48 (*Kojiki* 80; *Z* 227)
Songs 48 and 49 are both identified by the musical name: *Hina-buri no age-uta*, evidently a variation on the music called *Hina-buri* (*age-uta* meaning "rising song").
This song contains a play on words; the word *tashi-dashi* (anciently *tasi-dasi*) must be both an onomatopoeia for the sound of the hail as well as an adverb meaning something like "to the full."

49 (*Kojiki* 81; *Z* 228)
Like many of the ancient songs in the *tanka* form, this song has identical second and fifth lines.

50 (*Kojiki* 84; *Nihon Shoki* 71; *Z* 231)

Like songs 2 and 32, identified by the name *Amada-buri*.

See the note to song 2 for an explanation of the first two lines.

51 (*Kojiki* 92; *Z* 239)

This song is extremely similar in metrical form to song 151.

The word "rush-matting" (*tatami-komo*) is a *makura-kotoba* invariably applied to the geographical name Heguri, a place in Nara Prefecture.

52 (*Kojiki* 94; *Z* 241)

Song 77 was the first song given to her; both are identified as *Shitsu-uta*.

The last three lines could also mean: "When she was young / Would that I had slept with her— / But now she is old."

Hiketa is a place in Nara Prefecture; the old woman's name was Hiketa no Aka-iko.

53 (*Kojiki* 100; *Z* 245)

Evidently it was an old custom for the bride to run away and hide; such a practice is recorded as part of the marriage customs in parts of Okinawa.

54 (*Nihon Shoki* 92; *Z* 267)

See songs 231–240.

The *koto* is, of course, the *wagon*, or ancient Japanese harp.

55 (*Nihon Shoki* 93; *Z* 268)

The song revolves around the use of a pun; the word *tare* means both "hangs" and "anyone." The final two lines may also mean: "There is not anyone whom I love besides him."

Shitsu cloth seems to be cloth woven with a native Japanese design.

56 (*Nihon Shoki* 79; *Z* 270–271)

Both of them have puns on the two meanings of the word *tare*—"hang" and "anyone."

It has been suggested that this song is an elegy recorded here by mistake as a love song, a religious song of Mt. Mimoro (Mt. Miwa), or a song praising a lover.

The interpretation hinges on the meaning attached to the word "sigh"—in the original *nageku*, which would ordinarily mean "lament." No doubt the compilers of the *Nihon Shoki* understood the word to mean "sigh;" thus the fish came up and sighed at the beauty of the sight of the great lord.

If one accepts the interpretation as an elegy, the fish are lamenting in grief.

57 (*Hizen Fudoki*; *Z* 272)

The song does not fit the narrative especially well, and was probably an independent folk song of Hizen (modern Saga Prefecture.)

58 (*Nihon Shoki* 108; *Z* 83)

No doubt this was a woman's song, probably sung at an *utagaki* (*song contest*); the prophetic interpretation was attached later.

59 (*Nihon Shoki* 110; *Z* 85)

Song 193 is the first; songs 59 and 60 are the second and third. The latter two are given here because they deal unmistakably with love-making.

Song 59 was undoubtedly a song about rustic love-making to which was attached a prophetic significance. The song was supposed to prophesy the gentle disposition of the sons of Prince Shōtoku, who allowed themselves to be defeated by Soga-no-Iruka.

60 (*Nihon Shoki* 111; *Z* 86)

This is a song dealing with rustic love-making (perhaps a woman who spent the night with a strange man at an *utagaki*) to which was attached prophetic significance. Said to predict the sudden murder of Soga-no-Iruka (in 645 A.D.).

A *waza-uta* is a song which mysteriously came into the people's mouths in troubled times and which was believed to have a hidden, prophetic meaning. Some of the *waza-uta* seem to be political satire, and I have included them in that section; others seem to be ordinary folk songs or popular songs, as these.

61 (*Nihon Shoki* 115; *Z* 274)

The song expresses jealous concern.

62 (*Nihon Shoki* 128; *Z* 93)

(The others are 194 and 208).

Undoubtedly a popular love song meaning: "In such difficult circumstances, why bother to send messages? Better to act." Applied to the political situation, an exhortation to use direct action.

The identical song is found in the *Manyōshū* (no. 3069).

63 (*Hitachi Fudoki*; *Z* 278)

Manyōshū 3806 is a variant. Mount Wo-hatsuse is the famous Mount Hatsuse in Yamato. Evidently this is a folk song of Yamato which was handed down in Hitachi and came to be associated with this particular cave. The cave has been interpreted as meaning a tomb and the song as an invitation to double suicide. Probably the lovers are going into the cave merely to escape detection.

64 (*Hitachi Fudoki*; *Z* 279)

These are songs connected with the famous *utagaki* of Mount Tsukuba. An *utagaki* was a song contest between men and women, evidently followed by sexual promiscuity. The *Manyōshū* also contains songs dealing with the *utagaki* of Mount Tsukuba (nos. 1759–1760).

65 (*Hitachi Fudoki*; *Z* 280)

This is a song of self-derision by one who has not found a partner at the *utagaki*—probably sung collectively rather than by any individual.

66 (*Hitachi Fudoki*; *Z* 281)

This song consists largely of repetitions of the verbs *yosu* and *yoru*, both meaning "to approach," "to go near." This is the same verb translated as "to come towards" in song 1.

67 (*Hitachi Fudoki*; *Z* 282)

The last line has also been interpreted as meaning: "Even though she be an ugly, low-class maiden."

68 (*Hitachi Fudoki*; *Z* 283)

For *yū* cloth, see the explanation in the notes to song 94.

69 (*Hitachi Fudoki*; *Z* 284)

Tide: i.e., the throngs.

Last line: or, "I knew you because you looked at me."

70 (*Kogo Shūi*; *Z* 1)

71 (*Nihon Shoki* 16; *Z* 18)
Songs 71 and 72 are believed to be songs used in religious ceremonies at the Shrine of Mount Miwa (today called Ō-miwa Jinja).

72 (*Nihon Shoki* 17; *Z* 19)
Merely a variant of the preceding song.

73 (*Kogo Shūi*; *Kagura-uta*; *Z* 22)
The *Kagura-uta* contains another version of the song, sung in two parts:

> The great formal robes
> Of the priests
> Hanging below their knees—
>
> Hanging below their knees,
> How excellent as they wear them,
> The great formal robes.

All of the versions of the song present considerable difficulties of interpretation; this is another case in which slight phonetic changes bring about important changes in meaning.

The word translated as "priests" (*miya-bito*; in other documents, *ō-miya-bito*) may also mean "courtiers."

74 (*Kōtai Jingū Gishiki Chō*; *Z* 152)

75 (*Kōtai Jingū Gishiki Chō*; *Z* 153)
This song appears to be a variation based on the preceding song.
The word translated "courtiers" (here *ō-miya-bito*) may also mean "priests."

76 (*Kinkafu*; *Z* 156)
It may have been a song performed while using a willow branch as a magic implement to summon down a deity—thus the willow branch is called a "fore-runner" of the god.
The meaning of the first line is entirely unknown.
Ōhirume: another name of the Sun Goddess Ama-terasu-ō-mikami.

77 (*Kojiki* 93; *Z* 240)
Like song 52, this song is identified by the musical name *Shitsu-uta*.
Interpreted as a religious song of Mt. Miwa, referring to the sacred, untouchable nature of the virgin priestesses of the god who dwell in the oak forest. Also may be an *utagaki* song taunting reluctant maidens by saying they are as unapproachable as a sacred oak forest.

78 (*Kojiki* 95; *Kinkafu*; *Z* 242)
Also identified as *Shitsu-uta*.
The meaning is difficult to grasp, and the song has been subjected to various interpretations.
In the *Kinkafu* notation, only the first three lines are actually sung, and the third line is repeated four additional times.
The second song of reply by the old woman is song 190.

79 (*Kojiki* 97; *Z* 244)
Appears to be a religious song sung to accompany dancing.
The final line means literally: "Would that this were the Eternal World!"

80 (*Kinkafu*; *Honchō Getsurei*; *Z* 96)

The account is given by the *Honchō Getsurei*, and quoted in the *Nenchū Gyōji Hishō*.

The *Go-sechi* dance was a dance by five maidens performed every year at the *Shinjō-e*, the harvest festival in the eleventh month, and at the *Daijō-e*, the first harvest festival following the coronation of each Emperor.

The *Kinkafu* identifies the song with the musical name *Mijika-haniyasu-buri* ("Short *Haniyasu* Piece"). The *Kinkafu* notation makes it clear that the song was sung in two stanzas of slightly different but generally similar melodic pattern:

> The maidens,
> In order to act maiden-like,
> Wind jewels of Kara, *we ya*
>
> Jewels of Kara
> Around their wrists
> And act maiden-like.

Kara is China or the Asiatic continent in general.

81 (*Shoku Nihongi*; *Z* 104)

Similar to song 91. The same song is recorded, with numerous repetitions and refrains, in the *Saibara*; and the *Kokinshū* contains a similar song.

82 (*Kokinshū*; *Z* 312)

It was probably a traditional congratulatory song sung in the Court in the spring or at coronations.

As in so many early *tanka*, the second and fifth verse are identical.

83 (*Shoku Nihongi*; *Z* 14)

The same words appear also in a *chōka* in the *Manyōshū* by Ōtomo-no-Yakamochi (no. 4094), also written in the year 749.

Similar words were set to music and used as a military march in Japan during the Second World War.

84 (*Hitachi Fudoki*; *Z* 5)

The original text is in 4-syllable Chinese verse which is easier to translate into English than to reconstruct into ancient Japanese. Because the Chinese original observes a proper rhyming scheme, it may not be a direct translation of a Japanese original, but at any rate is valuable material for the study of ancient Japanese blessing formulas.

85 (*Kojiki* 101; *Z* 246)

The concept of song being able to pacify the irate spirit of the ruler is frequently met with in ancient songs; according to Professor Origuchi, *tama-shizume* or *chinkon* (spirit-pacification) was one of the basic rites of ancient Japanese religion, and one in which magic songs figured prominently.

This song is identified as *Ama-gatari-uta*; like songs 98 and 114, which also bear this musical name, the song ends in the same formula as the *Kamu-gatari* (songs 4–8). Like the *Kamu-gatari*, the *Ama-gatari-uta* are believed to have been part of the heritage of songs handed down by the Amabe clan.

This particular song is singled out for special praise by Tachibana Moribe (1781–1849), the Edo period scholar.

Hishiro is the name of the palace of Emperor Keikō in Makimuku; does not fit the narrative, which attributes it to the reign of Emperor Yūryaku.

Makimuku is the name of a place in Nara Prefecture; the narrative has the scene as Hatsuse, not Makimuku.

Hi is the same as modern Japanese *hinoki*, Japanese cypress.

Tsuki is the modern *keyaki* tree, *Zelkowa serrata Makino.*

Silken garments: a *makura-kotoba* for Mie; because Mie means literally "triple layers."

The lines about the water churning about are reminiscent of the *Kojiki* creation story, in which the deities Izanagi and Izanami churn the water with the tip of a jeweled spear and create the island of Onogoro.

86 (*Kojiki* 72; *Nihon Shoki* 62; *Z* 49)

The wild geese in Japan breed on the Asiatic or North American continents and come to Japan for the winter. It is very rare for them to lay eggs in Japan.

This series of three songs (85–87) is indentified by the musical name *Hoki-uta* (literally, "blessing songs"); the songs were obviously sung with congratulatory intent.

I have given here the *Nihon Shoki* version.

87 (*Kojiki* 73; *Nihon Shoki* 63; *Z* 50)

Any unusual event was regarded as an omen or sign by the ancient Japanese court; thus, the fact that a wild goose had laid an egg in Japan was considered an auspicious omen.

I have given here the *Kojiki* version.

88 (*Kojiki* 74; *Z* 51)

This song, omitted by the *Nihon Shoki*, is identified by the name *Hoki-uta no kata-uta*, and is in *kata-uta* form. It is considered to form an integral part of the preceding song and may be an early example of an envoy (*hanka*).

The second line is also interpreted as meaning: "Should know minutely." The other rendering seems more appropriate.

89 (*Nihon Shoki*, unnumbered)

Although usually not considered to be verse, this formula is of sufficient interest to be included here. The first paragraph is a magical formula imparting blessings on the lord of the house by analogy with various portions of the house. The second paragraph contains an invitation to drink; and the final paragraph seems to have something to do with a deer-dance, a common performance in ancient Japan.

Since this formula is believed to be an authentic house-blessing formula of great antiquity, it is among the oldest extant Japanese ritual formulas and is one of the most basic materials for the study of ancient Japanese religion.

90 (*Nihon Shoki* 83; *Z* 67)

Songs 263–265 are connected with different versions of the same story.

Although the religious character of this song is not as conspicuous as that of the house-blessing formula, it is usually considered to be a song of blessing of a general nature; the tenacity of the willow-tree is singled out for praise. In connection with the narrative, it of course hints at the unchanging identity of the two princes.

91 (*Kinkafu*; *Z* 162)

Identified in the *Kinkafu* by the name *Kata-oroshi*.

Song 94 is also identified as *Kata-oroshi*.

This song is quite similar to song 81 and to the *ō-naobi no uta* of the *Kokinshū* (no. 1069);

Manyōshū no. 815 (which is dated 730 A.D.) seems to be based on this song, and thus we can surmise with some justification that this song dates from before 730.

92 (*Shoku Nihongi*; *Z* 118)

Scholars are agreed that this *utagaki* was influenced by the imported Chinese custom of *tōka* (literally, "stamp-singing"), which was performed by rows of men and women singing and stamping their feet. In the late Nara period this custom became confused with the native *utagaki*.

Stamping the feet—the so-called *hembai*—is often found as a magical action in ancient sources; although magical significance is no longer consciously attached to it, it is still found in practically all Japanese dances and theatrical performances.

The palace: at Yugi in Kawachi.

93 (*Shoku Nihongi*; *Z* 119)

The wording of the *Shoku Nihongi* makes it clear that this and the preceding songs were the only songs newly composed for the occasion, and that song 92 was a preliminary blessing song, while this was one of the songs connected with the actual *utagaki* performance.

Hakata River: in present Ōsaka.

94 (*Kinkafu*; *Kagura-uta*; *Z* 154)

The same words appear twice in the *Kinkafu*, each time with a different musical name: *Kata-oroshi* and *Ō-naobi-uta*. Also appears in the *Kagura-uta*.

Yū: a cloth made of plant fibers hung on branches of plants in religious ceremonies; the words "*yū* cloth hanging" (*yū-shide no*) modify the word "god" (*kami*).

"All together:" in plenty?

"In particular:" without mishap or fault?

95 (*Kojiki* 7; *Nihon Shoki* 2; *Kakyō Hyōshiki*; *Z* 3)

The *Nihon Shoki* account adds that the brilliance of his form shone across two hills and two valleys, and those gathered at the funeral sang this song; or, his younger sister sang this song to inform those gathered at the funeral that this brilliance belonged to Aji-shiki-Taka-hikone.

The deity of this narrative has been identified as a lightning god; the meaning of the song becomes apparent only when considering it in this light.

Identified in both *Kojiki* and *Nihon Shoki* as *Hina-buri*.

The *Nihon Shoki* account follows this song with song 1, also identified as *Hina-buri*.

96 (*Kojiki* 48; *Z* 44)

This song is recorded in the *Kojiki* directly after songs 36–39.

The Kuzu were an aboriginal people inhabiting the upper reaches of the Yoshino River. Their way of life is described in the *Nihon Shoki* under the 19th year of the reign of Emperor Ōjin.

This and song 121 were both by the Kuzu and are typical songs of tribute by which a conquered people would express allegiance to the central court.

The words of the song have many interpretations. Chamberlain, following Tachibana Moribe, renders: "Sharp is the beginning, freezing is the end of the sword girded on Oho-sazaki, Oho-sazaki, the solar august child of Homuda,—[it is] chilly, chilly like the trees beneath the trunks of the winter trees."

Saya saya is an onomatopoeia depicting either the waving motion or the rustling sound of the plant.

Homuda is Emperor Ōjin, the father of Prince Ō-sazaki.

97 (*Kojiki* 58; *Nihon Shoki* 53; *Z* 205)

Like song 11, this song is identified by the musical term *Shitsu-uta no utai-kaeshi*. Other songs connected with this narrative are songs 279–283.

A song of praise of the Emperor, showing magical qualities.

I have given here the *Kojiki* version.

98 (*Kojiki* 102; *Z* 247)

It is also identified by the musical name *Ama-gatari-uta*.

The similarities to song 97 are conspicuous. Both are antique songs giving semi-divine praise to the ruler, and both seem to be deeply colored by magico-religious elements.

99 (*Kojiki* 105; *Z* 250)

(Following song 122.)

This song is identified by the musical name *Shitsu-uta*.

The words "Oh my brother!" here and elsewhere are a refrain (in the original *A-se wo*) and are not to be taken literally.

There are many cases in ancient Japanese verse where love songs or laudatory songs express the wish for some intimate connection or to become some article handled by the beloved. For example, the *Kagura-uta* contains the following song:

> Would that I were
> An offering (*mi-te-gura*)—
> Then, taken in the hands
> Of the sovereign deity,
> I would indulge in affectionate intimacies,
> I would indulge in affectionate intimacies!

100 (*Nihon Shoki* 78; *Z* 61)

This is another example of song and music being used to pacify the spirit of an enraged ruler.

The purpose of this song is similar to that of song 261.

Here is a paraphrase of the essential meaning of the song: "Would that my life were as long as the endless branches of the field of Ise—long that I might faithfully serve my lord: this is what the poor carpenter said."

"Until they are gone:" that is, until these endless branches should wither.

101 (*Nihon Shoki* 102; *Z* 76)

"Heaven" refers eulogistically to the palace in which the Empress dwells.

102 (*Nihon Shoki* 103; *Z* 77)

Ma is a eulogistic prefix.

Himuka: probably the same as present Hyūga.

Kure: China.

103 (*Shoku Nihongi*; *Z* 106)

Following song 111.

The author to whom songs 103 and 104 are attributed is not clear. Both are songs of praise of the Emperor connected with drinking wine.

I have, with some misgiving, uniformly translated the ancient Japanese word *toyo-miki* as "abundant wine," although the word *toyo* probably is endowed with richer, magico-religious nuances.

104 (*Shoku Nihongi*; *Z* 107)

105 (*Kojiki* 31; *Nihon Shoki* 22; *Z* 28)

The *Nihon Shoki* records them in a different order: 107, 105, 106.

However, both the *Kojiki* and *Nihon Shoki* agree in identifying them with the name *Kuni-shinohi-uta* (Land-recalling songs). They are intended to be songs of nostalgic praise for the land of Yamato.

106 (*Kojiki* 32; *Nihon Shoki* 23; *Z* 29)

This song is widely interpreted as a folk song to accompany some rural festival celebration. It has been suggested that it is the song of an elderly person approvingly urging youths to enjoy themselves. The wearing of the oak leaves must have been a festival custom.

107 (*Kojiki* 33; *Nihon Shoki* 21, *Z* 30)

This song is identified in the *Kojiki* as *Kata-uta*, and in the *Nihon Shoki* as *Kuni-shinohi-uta*. It is of course in the *Kata-uta* metrical form.

108 (*Kinkafu*; *Z* 32)

The *Kinkafu* identifies this song as the *Yomi-uta* (other *Yomi-uta* are songs 21 and 22) for the first day of the New Year.

A typical court song praising a country (*kuni-bome*).

There are certain discrepancies between the two versions in the *Kinkafu*; I have chosen here the version under the title, rather than that in the musical notation.

109 (*Kojiki* 42; *Nihon Shoki* 34; *Z* 43)

A typical example of a "land-viewing" (*kuni-mi*) song.

110 (*Nihon Shoki* 77; *Z* 60)

As mentioned before, Hatsuse is the modern Hase region in Nara Prefecture, famous for its old temple Hase-dera.

111 (*Shoku Nihongi*; *Z* 105)

Followed by songs 103 and 104.

112 (*Kojiki* 1; *Nihon Shoki* 1; *Z* 2)

Since it is the first song in both the *Kojiki* and *Nihon Shoki*, this song has traditionally been regarded as the earliest Japanese poem.

Believed to have originally been a song of blessing for a new house.

I give below, first in ancient and then in modern transcription, the Japanese text. Note the repetition of the word *yae-gaki* ("many-fenced palace").

Ya-kumo tatu	Ya-kumo tatsu
Idumo yafe-gaki	Izumo yae-gaki
Tuma-gömï ni	Tsuma-gomi ni
Yafe-gaki tukuru	Yae-gaki tsukuru
Sono yafe-gaki wo	Sono yae-gaki

113 (*Nihon Shoki* 24; *Z* 31)

Mikè can also be interpreted as meaning "sacred tree." The *makura-kotoba* "of the morning frost" perhaps applies to the word Mikè because of the other meaning of *mikè* as "august food"—because the Emperor's breakfast was carried across in the frosty morning chill.

114 (*Kojiki* 103; *Z* 248)

This song is also identified as an *Ama-gatari-uta*.

A song praising the life of the Court; the comparisons of the appearance of the courtiers with that of different species of birds seem rather absurd to us.

"Tails" evidently means their trains.

115 (*Nihon Shoki* 84; *Z* 70)

Oshinumi is a place in Nara Prefecture.

Songs 89–90 and 263–265 are also connected with the story of princes Oke and Woke.

Line 2: literally, that which I wish to see.

116 (*Nihon Shoki* 15; *Z* 17)

A typical wine-praising song, making use of the tradition of denying the private nature of the wine and attributing the responsibility for the wine to some deity, and concluding with a congratulatory refrain wishing longevity on the participants.

Ō-mono-nushi is, of course, the god Ya-chi-hoko or Ō-kuni-nushi, worshipped today at the shrine of Izumo. He and the god Sukuna-bikona cooperated in the building of the land and were revered as gods of medicine and wine—which were, indeed, all the same to the ancient Japanese (the word *kushi*, meaning wine, is related to the word *kusuri*, meaning medicine, and both are related etymologically to the adjective *kusushi*, meaning wondrous or marvelous).

117 (*Kojiki* 40; *Nihon Shoki* 32; *Kinkafu*; *Z* 41)

Identified by the name *Saka-hokahi no uta* in the *Kojiki* and *Kinkafu*; this name may be read *Saka-kura no uta*.

The *Kinkafu* makes it clear that this and the following song were performed at the *Tōka no sechie*, the court performance of *tōka* (see note to song 92) on the 16th day of the New Year.

Here the successful brewing of the wine is attributed, not to Ō-mono-nushi, but to his helper the god Sukuna-bikona.

118 (*Kojiki* 41; *Nihon Shoki* 33; *Kinkafu*; *Z* 42)

I have chosen the version of the *Kojiki*.

The drum mentioned here (the *tsuzumi*) is a hand-drum shaped somewhat like a spool; when turned on its side, it would resemble to some extent a tall, hollow mortar.

119 (*Kojiki* 50; *Z* 46)

This song is close to the *sedōka* metrical form.

120 (*Hitachi Fudoki*; *Z* 122)

121 (*Kojiki* 49; *Nihon Shoki* 39; *Z* 45)

The *Nihon Shoki* has a different account. When the Emperor Ōjin visited Yoshino in 288 A.D., the Kuzu came to him and sang this song while presenting wine. When they had finished singing, they clacked their mouths and laughed, which practice is still followed by them when they sing this song on presenting their local produce at the Court.

At least both accounts agree that the song was performed by the Kuzu when they came to the Court and presented their local products to the Emperor.

122 (*Kojiki* 104; *Kinkafu*; *Z* 249)

The *Kinkafu* records both this account and another extremely improbable account, by which a concubine of Emperor Yūryaku sang this song in sorrow seeing the Emperor killing her father.

According to the *Kinkafu*, this song was performed in the Court on the first day of the New Year. Both the *Kojiki* and *Kinkafu* call the song by the name *Uki-uta* ("wine-cup song").

The musical notation of the *Kinkafu* shows that the song was actually sung in two stanzas of six verses each, both to the same melody.

Line 1 is a *makura-kotoba* for the word "court noble" (*omi*), probably because of the phonetic similarities between *umi* (ocean) and *omi* (court noble).

123 (*Yakushi-ji Tablet* 1; *Z* 124)

This song expresses the wish that the merit gained by reproducing the relic reach the heavens and shake the earth, contributing to the salvation of the deceased ancestors and of all men.

124 (*Yakushi-ji Tablet* 2; *Z* 125)

The "thirty and two beautiful forms and eighty lovely appearances" are translations of Chinese terms frequently appearing in Buddhist works referring to the various ideal beauties found in each part of the form of the Buddha.

125 (*Yakushi-ji Tablet* 3; *Z* 126)

126 (*Yakushi-ji Tablet* 4; *Z* 127)

127 (*Yakushi-ji Tablet* 5; *Z* 128)

The original foot-prints of the Buddha were believed to be preserved in India. As a person able to produce foot-prints on solid rock, the Buddha is regarded here as endowed with supernatural powers. The foot-prints on the stone in Yakushi-ji Temple are those of a giant; the ancient Japanese, we can well believe, regarded the maker of the foot-prints as a sort of superman.

128 (*Yakushi-ji Tablet* 6; *Z* 129)

Here the Buddha is characterized by the term *masurawo* (the ideal of virile, intrepid manhood).

129 (*Yakushi-ji Tablet* 7; *Z* 130)

130 (*Yakushi-ji Tablet* 8; *Z* 131)

131 (*Yakushi-ji Tablet* 9; *Z* 132)

The latter-day Buddha is understood to mean the Buddhist Messiah Miroku (Maitreya), who will appear on earth billions of years after Sakyamuni and bring final deliverance to all beings. The foot-prints are to be preserved worshipfully and presented then as an offering to Miroku.

132 (*Yakushi-ji Tablet* 10; *Z* 133)

Between this song and song 133, there is one more song on the tablet which has become almost completely effaced.

133 (*Yakushi-ji Tablet* 12; *Z* 134)

134 (*Yakushi-ji Tablet* 13; *Z* 135)

135 (*Yakushi-ji Tablet* 14; *Z* 136)

136 (*Yakushi-ji Tablet* 15; *Z* 137)

Usually the meaning is interpreted as follows: "The ordinary doctors of this world heal usual human bodily ills, but the newly arrived healer from abroad, he who saves the world from all its woes, is the healer truly holy and rare." Another interpretation is that the "usual healers" are the native Japanese gods, such as Ōnamuchi (another name for Ō-kuni-nushi) and Sukuna-bikona, who were anciently invoked as the patrons of medicine and the healers of sickness. Thus this song would praise the powers of Buddhist healing to the detriment of the native Japanese gods. The successes of the foreign medical knowledge which was imported to Japan in connection with Buddhism contributed greatly to the rapid spread of Buddhism in Japan.

137 (*Yakushi-ji Tablet* 16; *Z* 138)

138 (*Yakushi-ji Tablet* 17; *Z* 139)
   In this song, Buddhism appears as a salvation religion, offering remission of sin by the use of holy relics.

139 (*Yakushi-ji Tablet* 18; *Z* 140)
   This is the first of the four final songs entitled "Reprimands on Life and Death."
   The idea that it is not an easy matter to be born as a human being is frequently emphasized in Buddhist writings, and a poem in the *Manyōshū* written some 24 years before (no. 1785) has the same idea.

140 (*Yakushi-ji Tablet* 19; *Z* 141)
   The "four serpents" are the four elements—earth, water, fire, and wind—of which all matter is composed.
   The "five ghosts" are usually interpreted as the five accumulations—perceptible forms, sense impressions, thoughts, actions, and cognitions—the five components of mental activity in Buddhist philosophy.

141 (*Yakushi-ji Tablet* 20; *Z* 142)

142 (*Yakushi-ji Tablet* 21; *Z* 143)
   Portions of this song are illegible; I have followed Kimoto, who in his *Jōdai kayō shōkai*, has supplied a clever reconstruction (p. 136).

143 (*Tōdaiji Yōroku*; *Z* 108)
   Rusana is the Buddha Vairocana, also known in Japanese as Dainichi Nyorai.
   "East:" east of Nara.

144 (*Tōdaiji Yōroku*; *Z* 109)

145 (*Tōdaiji Yōroku*; *Z* 110)
   Gangoji, also called Asuka-dera, was located in Asuka in Nara Prefecture and was one of the first—if not the first—centers of Buddhism in Japan.

146 (*Kojiki* 34; *Z* 289)
   Strictly speaking, a dying-song rather than an elegy. Expresses regretful longing.

147 (*Kojiki* 35; *Z* 290)
   It has been suggested that this song is not a song of mourning, but, for example, a love song. However, the *Kojiki* text plainly states that songs 147–150 were sung at Imperial funerals; the songs themselves contain no elements disqualifying them as elegies; and they fit the prose narrative surprisingly well.
   Tokoro is a kind of wild potato: *Dioscorea tokoro Makino*.
   The final line has been subjected to a variety of interpretations. My rendition is tentative.

148 (*Kojiki* 36; *Z* 291)

149 (*Kojiki* 37; *Z* 292)

150 (*Kojiki* 38; *Z* 293)

The *Kojiki* follows this sequence of four songs with the note that they were sung at the funerals of the Emperors.

The actual wording of this song is as follows: "The plovers of the beach / Do not go by the sandy beaches. . . ." I have here understood it figuratively.

151 (*Kojiki* 52; *Nihon Shoki* 43; *Z* 294)
(Follows after song 246.)
Seems not to fit the narrative. Although literally the song speaks of cutting down trees for bow-wood, there are unmistakable overtones hinting at killing, and the song thus has a double meaning.

Tachibana Moribe singles this song out for praise as one of the three or four greatest songs in this body of verse. However, the difficulties of interpretation inevitably detract somewhat from the value.

Quite close in metrical form to song 51.

Azusa is the catalpa tree, used widely as material for bows.

Mayumi is the *Euonymus Sieboldianus Blume*, also used for bows.

152 (*Nihon Shoki* 94; *Z* 295)
The first ten lines are devoted to a lengthy enumeration of the places through which Kage-hime passed—each place name accompanied by a *makura-kotoba*. The objectivity of the diction makes it probable that the song was not sung by Kage-hime herself, but was either a song about her or a sort of dramatic aria accompanying her actions.

Long enumerations of places through which a hero passed are common in later literature; in the theater they are called *michi-yuki*. The *Manyōshū* contains examples of them (nos. 43, 3230, 3236, 3237, 3240).

Evidently carrying rice and water was part of a funeral ceremony.

153 (*Nihon Shoki* 95; *Z* 296)
This song has also been interpreted as a song sung when Shibi was hiding in the mountains, rather than a song of mourning after his death.

154 (*Nihon Shoki* 98; *Z* 297)
The song reads as if the dead man were himself playing the flute. Music of flutes was evidently used at funeral ceremonies.

Hirakata: name of a place on the Yodo-gawa river in present-day Ōsaka.

155 (*Jōgū Shōtoku Hōō Teisetsu*; *Z* 298)
Ikaruga is believed to be the vicinity of present Hōryūji village.

156 (*Jōgū Shōtoku Hōō Teisetsu*; *Z* 299)
This song is given also in various other sources, in some as emanating from the starving person (identified later as a supernatural being) on whom the Prince had pity (see song 271).

157 (*Jōgū Shōtoku Hōō Teisetsu*; *Z* 300)
The exact meaning of this song is not clear.

158 (*Jōgū Shōtoku Hōō Teisetsu*; *Z* 301)
The meaning is: "Would that I could say that all this about your passing away was all a lie, as unfounded and empty as the skies in which are towering the trees on the mountains of Ikaruga."

159 (*Nihon Shoki* 113; *Z* 302)
This and the following song are attributed to the scribe (*fuhito* means scribe) and can

probably be accepted as actually having been written by him. The author was evidently a descendant of continental immigrants and can be supposed to have been familiar with classical Chinese literature. A certain similarity has been noted between this song and the first song in the *Shih ching*, the ancient Chinese "Book of Songs."

160 (*Nihon Shoki* 114; *Z* 303)

This song is strikingly similar to no. 4323 in the *Manyōshū*. Here are the originals of both:

NIHON SHOKI	MANYŌSHŪ
Moto-goto ni	Toki-doki no
Hana wa sakedomo	Hana wa sakedomo
Nani to ka mo	Nani sure so
Utsukushi imo ga	Haha tofu hana no
Mata saki-de konu	Saki-de kozu-kemu

The meaning of the *Manyōshū* poem is as follows: "The flowers of each season / Bloom, / But why is it / That the flower called "Mother" / Will not bloom forth?" Attributed to a border guard.

161 (*Nihon Shoki* 116; *Z* 304)

The song means: "If only a cloud were to rise visibly above the hill where he is buried, then at least I would feel somewhat consoled—but there is nothing!"

These songs are all contemporary with the early *Manyō* era, and there is a marked similarity in tone. For instance, the same idea is expressed in poems no. 225 and 2452 of the *Manyōshū*.

162 (*Nihon Shoki* 117; *Z* 305)

The meaning is that the Prince was wise beyond his years, so that the Empress never thought of him as being a mere child. Similar in diction to *Manyōshū* no. 3874.

163 (*Nihon Shoki* 118; *Z* 306)

This type of figurative expression is widely employed in the *Manyōshū*.

164 (*Nihon Shoki* 119; *Z* 307)

Imaki, the place where the Prince was interred, was evidently where he lived together with the Empress.

165 (*Nihon Shoki* 120; *Z* 308)

The original of the song is conspicuous in its use of alliteration: the vowel *u* appears at the beginning of three of the five lines and also within four lines:

> Minato no
> Ushio no kudari
> Una kudari
> Ushiro mo kure ni
> Okite ka yukamu

166 (*Nihon Shoki* 121; *Z* 309)

The Empress entrusted these songs to the naturalized Chinese Hata-no-Ōkura-no-Miyatsuko-Maro, commanding him to hand them on and not to allow them to be forgotten.

The *Manyōshū* contains several songs (nos. 9, 10, 11, 12) written by *Manyō* poets at the time of the Empress' visit to the hot-springs of Ki.

167 (*Nihon Shoki* 123; *Z* 310)

168 (*Nippon Ryōiki*; *Z* 111)

I have adopted the figurative interpretation; actually, all that is literally said in the original is:

> That old liar bird,
> The crow
> In words only
> Said "Together,"
> But went on ahead.

169 (*Kojiki* 11; *Nihon Shoki* 9; *Z* 7)

In the *Nihon Shoki*, the song is sung by Michi-no-omi at Emperor Jimmu's command as a signal to strike the enemy (here remnants of the Emishi warriors) at a banquet to which they had been lured.

In the *Nihon Shoki* this song follows song 174.

Here I have followed the version given in the *Kojiki*.

Songs 169–175 are identified by the name *Kume-uta* ("Kume songs") and were handed on by a clan of warriors called Kume.

170 (*Nihon Shoki* 10; *Z* 8)

Together with song 70, this is one of the most primitive of any of the songs in this volume, consisting almost entirely of short exclamations.

171 (*Nihon Shoki* 11; *Kakyō Hyōshiki*; *Z* 9)

The Emishi have been identified—with what certainty, I do not know—with the Ainu.

172 (*Kojiki* 12; *Nihon Shoki* 13; *Z* 10)

The *Nihon Shoki*, on the other hand, attributes them to Emperor Jimmu, who sang them in a desire for revenge against Naga-sune-hiko, who had killed the Emperor's brother Prince Itsuse in the battle of Kusaka.

I have given the *Kojiki* version.

173 (*Kojiki* 13; *Nihon Shoki* 14; *Z* 11)

The word which I translated as "pepper plant" may mean "ginger" instead.

174 (*Kojiki* 14; *Nihon Shoki* 8; *Z* 12)

The *Nihon Shoki* has it that Emperor Jimmu sang it, confident of victory, before he engaged the enemy in battle at Mount Kuni-mi.

I have chosen the *Nihon Shoki* version, which contains all the repetitions and refrains which are omitted in the abbreviated *Kojiki* version.

175 (*Kojiki* 15; *Nihon Shoki* 12; *Z* 13)

176 (*Nihon Shoki* 28; *Z* 37)

The "lord of Uchi" refers to Takeshi-Uchi-no-sukune. The idea of the lines about grains of sand in his belly must be: "What is there to be afraid of about the lord of Uchi?"

177 (*Kojiki* 39; *Nihon Shoki* 29; *Z* 38)

178 (*Nihon Shoki* 30; *Z* 39)

179 (*Nihon Shoki* 31; *Z* 40)

180 (*Nihon Shoki* 82; *Z* 65)

The word in the third verse here translated as "mother" *(amo)* may be read *ame* ("heaven") instead. In this case, the meaning would be as follows:

> The lad Woshiro,
>> Fighting on the road!
> Though his fame
>> May not reach the heavens,
> Let his fame
>> Be made known on earth!

181 (*Kojiki* 10; *Nihon Shoki* 7; *Z* 6)

The song evidently has not the slightest connection with the narrative. Uda was known as a hunting region, and because the historical narrative had the Uda district as its background, this song became attached to the narrative and was handed down by the Kume clan as one of their Kume-uta (see songs 169–175).

The song was evidently originally a jocular folk song about hunting; the shameless discrimination between the old wife and the new wife in the polygamous family is evidently intended to be humorous.

The word translated here as "whale" has also been interpreted as meaning "hawk."

182 (*Kojiki* 30; *Nihon Shoki* 27; *Z* 27)

I have here given the *Kojiki* version.

This song has been often considered to be a folk song of the land of Ise. Such songs of endearment for natural objects were often written by travelers in ancient Japanese literature.

183 (*Ise Fudoki*; *Z* 36)

There is a very close variant version of this song in the *Manyōshū* (no. 61). Believed to have been a folk song of Ise.

The song revolves around a pun: *mato,* the first portion of the geographical name Mato-kata, also means "target."

184 (*Harima Fudoki*; *Z* 47)

This song is in the *Bussoku-seki-ka* verse form (see p. 91).

I think that the fifth line *(na kare so ne)* is susceptible of double interpretation: "Do not wither" and "Do not depart." The verb *karu* has these two meanings.

185 (*Kinkafu*; *Z* 215)

The song is identified by the musical term *(Sitsu-uta no) utai-kaeshi.*

It is quite odd that the song should fit none of the three narratives given in the text. Undoubtedly it refers to a woman brought and "transplanted," so to speak, from the island of Awaji in the Inland Sea to Asatsuma (or Asazuma, a place in Nara Prefecture) —perhaps to serve at the court in Yamato.

186 (*Hizen Fudoki*; *Z* 285)

The song is, of course, a variant of the following song and of *Manyōshū* no. 385. This song is identified by the name *Kishima-buri,* and appears to be an *utagaki* song.

187 (*Kojiki* 70; *Z* 219)

For other songs preceding this in the same narrative, see songs 249–251.

188 (*Kojiki* 71; *Z* 220)

189 (*Nihon Shoki* 61; *Z* 221)

190 (*Kojiki* 96; *Z* 243)

This song is also identified as *Shitsu-uta*.

The song is one of envy of the young sung by an older person.

Kusaka is a place in present Ōsaka.

191 (*Nihon Shoki* 107; *Z* 81)

Two very fanciful interpretations of the song are recorded in the *Nihon Shoki*. Actually, it must have been simply a popular song.

Recorded also in two biographical works about Prince Shōtoku.

192 (*Shōtoku Taishi Denryaku*; *Jōgū Shōtoku Taishi Den Hoketsu-ki*; *Z* 82)

This song is extremely difficult to interpret. I do not know what type of a plant the *ude* is. Since water and metal are highly compatible elements in Chinese thought, the meaning has been conjectured to be: "coöperate with each other as if you were water and metal."

193 (*Nihon Shoki* 109; *Z* 84)

194 (*Nihon Shoki* 126; *Z* 91)

Yeshino: same as Yoshino.

Nagi, seri: both edible plants growing in shallow water.

195 (*Shoku Nihongi*; *Nippon Ryōiki*; *Saibara*; *Z* 117)

Slightly different versions are recorded in the *Nippon Ryōiki* and in the *Saibara* songs of the Heian period. I have given here the version of the *Shoku Nihongi*.

196 (*Nippon Kōki*; *Nippon Ryōiki*; *Z* 121)

The only connection with Prince Yabe is, of course, the geographical name Yabe. Other popular songs contain prohibitions against treading (see song 203).

197 (*Nippon Kōki*; *Z* 151)

The word *furu-uta* (*koka?*) may mean simply "old song." In this sense, the interpretation of the words *no-naka furu-michi* as "the old path through the fields" is unassailable.

Nevertheless it has been suggested that the word Furu was a place name (there is a place called Furu in Nara Prefecture) closely connected with Korean immigrants, and that this song might have been a traditional song handed down among the families of Korean extraction. In this case, it is possible that *furu-michi* may mean "path at Furu."

The exact sense of the song is also not clear.

198 (*Kinkafu*; *Z* 155)

Recorded in the *Kinkafu* under the name *Takahashi-buri*; there is no prose narrative attached.

It has been suggested that the *hari* (black alder, *Alnus japonica var. genuina Call.*) and *kunugi* (*Quercus serrata*) trees represent persons; thus the song may be poking fun cryptically at a couple who are on good terms with each other, or at roadside prostitutes.

I have given the version in the musical notation. The other version is shorn of its repetitions and refrains and given as a *tanka*:

> By the roadside,
> The *hari* and *kunugi* trees
> Are being coquettish,
> So it is said—
> The *hari* and *kunugi* trees.

"Coquettish:" also interpreted as "act pliant, lithesome," or "speak in hushed voices." The original is *shinameku*.

199 (*Kinkafu*; *Z* 157)
Recorded in the *Kinkafu* without prose narrative; the musical name, *Ame-hito-buri* is derived from the first word of the original, *Ame-hito* ("heavenly ones").

Extremely difficult of interpretation. Has been suggested to be a song expressing the discontent of the peasantry about agricultural labor.

"Heavenly ones:" *ame-hito*—literally, "heaven-men," also applied to the nobility.

"*Kawara, yura:*" the exact connotations of these onomatopoeia are not clear; evidently these lines depict the difficulty of tilling a rocky paddy.

200 (*Kinkafu*; *Z* 158)
Recorded in the *Kinkafu* without prose narrative. The musical name *Tsugi-ne-buri* is derived from the first word, the *makura-kotoba tsuginefu* (here translated "of the many mountain peaks").

It would seem that this is a parody on some serious love song.

201 (*Kinkafu*; *Z* 159)
Recorded in the *Kinkafu* without prose narrative. The musical name *Niwa-tachi-buri* (or *Niwa-ni-tatsu-buri*) is derived from the first line: *niwa ni tatsu* ("standing in the yard").

Numerous interpretations are possible. I interpret the bird of the first verse as a veiled reference to the lover, who is asked to come at night and awaken the maiden if she should drop off to sleep while waiting for him.

202 (*Kinkafu*; *Z* 160)
Recorded in the *Kinkafu* without prose narrative. The name *Afushite-buri* is derived from the first word *afushite* (here translated as "acorns").

Usually interpreted simply as a song offering acorns to one's aunt, or as expressing concern for the health of an ailing aunt. I sense some sexual overtones: "These acorns that I offer you won't keep, so let's enjoy them with pleasure, and then let's sleep together with pleasure." This type of interpretation seems more in keeping with the general characteristics of ancient Japanese songs.

"Acorns:" original, *afushite*, believed to be some kind of nut or acorn.

203 (*Kinkafu*; *Z* 161)
Recorded in the *Kinkafu* without prose narrative. The name *Yamakuchi-buri* is derived from the first word *yamakuchi* ("foot of the mountain").

Often interpreted as a prohibition against entering a sacred place. Song 196 also contains a prohibition against treading. Perhaps, like song 199, may be interpreted as having elements of popular protest.

204 (*Kinkafu*; *Z* 163)
Recorded in the *Kinkafu* without prose narrative. The musical name is *Naga-haniyasu-buri* ("Long *Haniyasu* Piece"). Song 80 is identified as *Mijika-haniyasu-buri*, or "Short *Haniyasu* Piece."

The meaning of the song is not at all clear; I follow one conjectured interpretation. The song was evidently performed on the first day of the New Year in the Court.

205 (*Nihon Shoki* 112; *Z* 87)

206 (*Nihon Shoki* 122; *Z* 88)
This is the most difficult song in the *Nihon Shoki*, entirely incomprehensible as it stands.

I have followed Tsuchihashi (*Kodai Kayō shū*, p. 205), who cleverly transposes various characters after the example of Keichū to obtain this interesting reading. As in song 210, the words of the text were no doubt purposely jumbled to conceal the criticism of the Empress implied. The song seems to say that Silla is laying waste the kingdom of Paekche because of the weakness of the Korean policy of the Japanese Court.

The fourth line is still hopelessly unintelligible.

207 (*Nihon Shoki* 125; *Z* 90)

It is not clear whether the song praises or derides the highly honored foreigners. The *tachibana*, or little wild orange, is a tree brought to Japan by continental immigrants and has miniature fruit which was strung on cords and worn as ornaments on the head. (See note to song 36.)

208 (*Nihon Shoki* 127; *Z* 92)

Interpreted as referring to the alacrity with which Prince Ō-ana (later Emperor Temmu rose to the occasion while the court nobles were unable to master the situation.

209 (*Nippon Ryōiki*; *Z* 113)

The questions about the clam and the flatfish are interpreted to mean: "When will that fellow like a clam die? When will that fellow like a flatfish die?

210 (*Nippon Ryōiki*; *Z* 114)

Because of the political implications, these songs are all written in cryptical fashion, making them difficult to read and interpret accurately. However, there is not the slightest doubt of the satirical intent and of the intended meaning.

Komo-zuchi: a weight used in weaving straw matting. Used here cryptically for penis.

211 (*Nippon Ryōiki*; *Z* 115)

Second of the songs sung throughout the country satirizing the scandalous sexual relations between Empress Kōken and the priest Dōkyō.

212 (*Nippon Ryōiki*; *Z* 116)

Another song sung during the second reign of Empress Kōken. Satirizes the fact that Dōkyō, the paramour of the Empress, was given the title of *Hōō*, or Pope, and another priest Inkō was given the title *Hōshin sangi*, or Priestly Adviser.

Evidently the song contains an invitation to bring in another fat priest to satisfy the Empress's lusts.

213 (*Kojiki* 16; *Z* 174)

214 (*Kojiki* 17; *Z* 175)

Songs 214–216 are all in the *kata-uta* verse form.

215 (*Kojiki* 18; *Z* 176)

No satisfactory explanation of the first two verses has been made. Perhaps the words are names of birds, or nonsense syllables.

The corners of the eye-lids were pierced and ink inserted to give the eyes a menacing look.

216 (*Kojiki* 19; *Z* 177)

217 (*Kinkafu*; *Z* 33)

These songs were sung in the Court on the 7th day of the New Year at the *Hakuba no sechie*, or Festival of the White Horse.

It has been suggested that these three songs may have originally been festival songs of the Takahashi region (near Nara).

Song 217 is the question song; and 218–219 are songs of reply.

218 (*Kinkafu*; *Z* 34)
Furu and Iso-no-kami (or Isu-no-kami) are place names near Takahashi in Nara Prefecture.

This song is based on a pun between the words *mu-tsuma* (six claws) and *mutsumashimi* (thinking fondly).

219 (*Kinkafu*; *Z* 35)

220 (*Kojiki* 26; *Nihon Shoki* 25; *Z* 25)

221 (*Kojiki* 27; *Nihon Shoki* 26; *Z* 26)
This pair of songs shows the high esteem in which were held those who could compose extemporaneous verse.

222 (*Kojiki* 28; *Owari no Kuni Atsuta Jingū Engi*; *Z* 284)
Professor Origuchi surmises that in ancient religion women became priestesses sacred to the gods during the menstrual period; thus, menstrual blood, far from being a defilement, was a sign of religious consecration. (*Nihon bungaku-shi nōto,* v. i, p. 102–113.)

"Moon has risen:" that is, menstrual blood has appeared.

223 (*Kojiki* 29; *Owari no Kuni Atsuta Jingū Engi*; *Z* 185)
An excellent example of ancient repartee.

In both this and the preceding song, I have given the versions found in the *Kojiki.*

224 (*Nihon Shoki* 44; *Z* 197)
This song is in the *kata-uta* form.

Last line: a *makura-kotoba* modifying the word *omi*, meaning "court noble."

225 (*Nihon Shoki* 45; *Z* 198)
Line 2: a *makura-kotoba* modifying Harima.

Line 4: a *makura-kotoba* modifying *kasikoku* ("full of awe").

226 (*Nihon Shoki* 46; *Z* 199)
"Noble:" here the Emperor.

227 (*Nihon Shoki* 47; *Z* 200)

228 (*Nihon Shoki* 48; *Z* 201)
The first three lines are a typical introductory passage, leading up to the central idea of the song—"to lay side by side."

229 (*Nihon Shoki* 49; *Z* 202)

230 (*Nihon Shoki* 50; *Z* 203)
Asazuma: a place in Nara Prefecture. Iwa-no-hime came from a family of this place.

231 (*Kojiki* 106; *Z* 256)

232 (*Kojiki* 107; *Z* 257)

233 (*Kojiki* 108; *Z* 258)
Evidently means: "Because your heart is slack and slovenly, you can't get inside my fence."

234 (*Kojiki* 109; *Nihon Shoki* 87; *Z* 259, 262)

235 (*Kojiki* 110; *Z* 260)
In the *Bussoku-seki-ka* verse form.

236 (*Kojiki* 111; *Z* 261)
The song makes use of the name of the girl Ofuwo ("Great Fish") and Shibi ("Tuna").

237 (*Nihon Shoki* 88; *Z* 263)

238 (*Nihon Shoki* 89; *Z* 264)
Last line: or, I intend to engage you in battle.

239 (*Nihon Shoki* 90; *Z* 265)
The meaning of the fourth line is not clear; this rendering is merely a guess.

240 (*Nihon Shoki* 91; *Z* 266)
Followed by songs 54–55, 152–153.

241 (*Tango Fudoki*; *Z* 123)
Song of the Angel of Manai, recorded in a fragment of the *Tango Fudoki* quoted in a book called *Ruijū Jingi Hongen* (1320 A.D.).

242 (*Kojiki* 23; *Nihon Shoki* 18; *Z* 20)
The *Nihon Shoki* has a slightly different version; I give here the *Kojiki* version.
Evidently understood as being a song pronounced oracularly by a young maiden.
Mimaki-iri-biko was a name of Emperor Sūjin.

243 (*Nihon Shoki* 19; *Z* 21)
The words of the song, according to which the rocks are being passed up the mountain, differ from the prose account.

244 (*Hitachi Fudoki*; *Z* 23)
The text seems to be corrupt, making any sensible interpretation almost impossible.

245 (*Kojiki* 24; *Nihon Shoki* 20; *Z* 24)

246 (*Kojiki* 51; *Nihon Shoki* 42; *Z* 48)
This song is followed by Prince Uji's elegy, song 151.

247 (*Harima Fudoki*; *Z* 52)
Recorded in a fragment of the *Harima Fudoki* quoted in the *Shaku Nihongi*, a commentary on the *Nihon Shoki*.
Sumi-no-e is a place name in Ōsaka (or Naniwa); Akashi is the place down the coast past present day Kōbe.

248 (*Kojiki* 75; *Nihon Shoki* 41; *Z* 53)
This song is identified as *Shitsu-uta no utai-kaeshi*.
The onomatopoetic words *saya saya* refer to both the clear sound of the *koto* and the languid motion of the underwater plants. The same words are used similarly at the end of song 96.

249 (*Kojiki* 67; *Z* 216)

250 (*Kojiki* 68; *Z* 217)
Hayabusa, the name of the prince, means a fierce bird of prey, in modern Japanese the peregrine falcon.
In the account given in the *Nihon Shoki*, when the Emperor visited Medori's quarters, her weaving maidens were singing the following song (*Nihon Shoki* 59):

The fruit of the heavenly
Metal loom,
The metal loom woven
By Medori,
Is cloth for a coat
For Hayabusa-wake.

251 (*Kojiki* 69; *Nihon Shoki* 60; *Z* 218)
The *Nihon Shoki* attributes the song to the attendants of Prince Hayabusa-wake.
I have given the *Kojiki* version of the song.
The wagtail (*sazaki*) refers to the Emperor Nintoku, whose name was Ō-sazaki.
These songs are followed by songs 187–189.

252 (*Kojiki* 76; *Z* 54)

253 (*Kojiki* 77; *Z* 55)
The traditional interpretation is:
On Hanifu hill
When I stood and looked,
In flames,
The houses were burning—
Where my wife's house stood.

254 (*Kojiki* 78; *Nihon Shoki* 64; *Z* 256)

255 (*Kojiki* 82; *Nihon Shoki* 72; *Z* 229)
The *Nihon Shoki* says that Prince Anaho sang this as a song greeting Ōmae-no-sukune.
It is not clear whether Ōmae and Womae are two individuals, or whether there is one person called Ōmae-Womae-no-sukune.

256 (*Kojiki* 83; *Nihon Shoki* 73; *Z* 230)
In the *Nihon Shoki*, Ōmae-no-sukune is recorded as having simply sung this song in reply.
The *Kojiki* identifies this song as *Miya-hito-buri*, from the first word *miya-hito* (noble courtier).
After this Prince Karu was surrendered to his captors; whereupon he sang songs 50, 2, etc.

257 (*Nihon Shoki* 74; *Z* 57)

258 (*Kojiki* 98; *Nihon Shoki* 75; *Z* 58)
I have given here the version of the *Kojiki*.
The purpose of the legend and song is to show that even insects obediently serve the Emperor. The incident of the dragon fly was no doubt regarded as an auspicious omen and immediately connected with the term "Dragon-fly Island," an ancient name for Japan.
Ancient literature abounds in these unconvincing accounts of the origin of geographical names.

259 (*Kojiki* 99; *Nihon Shoki* 76; *Z* 59)

260 (*Nihon Shoki* 79; *Z* 62)

261 (*Nihon Shoki* 80; *Z* 63)
The song is in the *sedōka* verse form.

262 (*Nihon Shoki* 81; *Z* 64)

The *Nihon Shoki* has an alternate version of the 4th line: "It would not have arrived in time."

263 (*Kojiki*; *Z* 66)

The song is called *hagame* (chant?) and, although poetic in diction, does not seem to be in any recognizable verse form. It is not written phonetically, as is all the verse in the *Kojiki*, and is capable of many readings.

This song is often given as an example of the loose association of ideas in ancient verse. There is only the vaguest connection between any of the ideas.

Izaho-wake: Emperor Richū, grandfather of the princes.

Oshi-ha: the father of the princes, never actually reigned.

264 (*Harima Fudoki*; *Z* 68)

The song contains a pun on *ta-utsu,* which means both "clap the hands" and "hoe a field."

265 (*Harima Fudoki*; *Z* 69)

266 (*Kojiki* 112; *Nihon Shoki* 85; *Z* 71)

267 (*Kojiki* 113; *Nihon Shoki* 86; *Z* 72)

268 (*Nihon Shoki* 99; *Z* 73)

The song is in the *sedōka* verse form.

Rather than a song of welcome, it seems to be more a song of anxiety for what is to come.

"Kara:" here, Korea.

269 (*Nihon Shoki* 100; *Z* 74)

270 (*Nihon Shoki* 101; *Z* 75)

Both 269 and 270 are really the same song, and both seem to be the work of a third party.

271 (*Nihon Shoki* 104; *Z* 78)

The song is also given in two biographies of Prince Shōtoku, which identify it by the name *Hina-buri.* Another version is recorded in the *Manyōshū* (no. 415).

272 (*Shōtoku Taishi Denryaku*)

Appears to be a song about the burning of the Palace of Ikaruga—which happened in 643 A.D., after the death of Prince Shōtoku. Probably it was attached to this story by mistake or in a prophetical sense.

273 (*Nihon Shoki* 105; *Z* 79)

274 (*Nihon Shoki* 106; *Z* 80)

Has also been interpreted as a song of contemporaries criticizing Soga-no-Emishi.

275 (*Kojiki* 21; *Z* 15)

These two *tanka,* the only purely descriptive nature poems in the whole body of verse, seem to symbolize uneasiness and foreboding.

276 (*Kojiki* 22; *Z* 16)

277 (*Kojiki* 54; *Z* 193)

Follows after song 29 and is followed by song 40.

Since the song contains no mention of love or yearning, I have included it in this section as an independent land-surveying song. An early example of the technique called *kuni-zukushi*, in which many geographical names are woven into the text.

278 (*Nihon Shoki* 51; *Z* 204)
Evidently bells were attached to horses and boats belonging to the Court.

279 (*Kojiki* 59; *Nihon Shoki* 54; *Z* 206)
This is another early example of *michi-yuki*, a recurrent style of Japanese verse which weaves numerous geographical names, often modified (as here) by their *makura-kotoba*, into the verse. See also song 152.
This song is identified as *Shitsu-uta no utai-kaeshi*.

280 (*Kojiki* 60; *Nihon Shoki* 52; *Z* 207)

281 (*Kojiki* 63; *Nihon Shoki* 55; *Z* 210)

282 (*Nihon Shoki* 56; *Z* 211)
The song is difficult to interpret, but I think that the statements about the mulberry branch apply figuratively to the Emperor. Thus:
"Iwa-no-hime does not speak generously of this poor mulberry branch; drifting down the river, constantly approaching the dangerous river bends, comes the poor mulberry branch."

283 (*Kojiki* 64; *Nihon Shoki* 57; *Z* 212)
Identified by the name *Shitsu-uta no utai-kaeshi*. The beginning is identical with that of song 11, which also has the same musical name.

284 (*Todaiji Yōroku*; *Z* 164)
The poem was probably written by a woman of high rank when presenting the scepter to her beloved.

285 (Document preserved at the Shōsō-in in Nara; *Z* 286)
The song is believed to have two meanings, based on a pun on the word *utsusu*, which can mean both "to dye" and "to copy." Thus, the poem also contains the meaning: "It has become difficult to copy any longer."

286 (*Kokinshū* 406; *Tosa Nikki*; *Z* 313)
Kasuga: a region in Nara Prefecture.

287 (*Kagura-uta*; *Shūi Waka Shū*; *Z* 314)
Because of the mention of the capital of Nara, the song is believed to have originated during the Nara period.

288 (*Saibara*; *Z* 315)
The translation does not contain the many exclamations and repetitions found in the original, which is as follows:

> *Sawada-gawa*
> *Sode tsuku bakari*
> > *Ya*
> *Asakeredo*
> > *Hare*
> *Asakeredo*
> *Kuni no miya-hito*
> > *Ya*

> *Takahashi watasu*
>   *Ahare*
>   *Soko yoshi ya*
> *Takahashi watasu*

The indented portions are all exclamations or refrains, not part of the main words.

289 (*Kakyō Hyōshiki*; Z 311)
The same song is contained in the *Manyōshū*: nos. 164; and no. 163 was also written on the same occasion.

290 (*Kakyō Hyōshiki*; Z 179)
The song is couched entirely in figurative language.

291 (*Kakyō Hyōshiki*; Z 180)
Evidently this is a song of modest acceptance.

292 (*Kakyō Hyōshiki*; Z 275)
However, the *Manyōshū* attributes the same poem (no. 505) to Abe-no-iratsume, a lady of the early-middle Nara period.
The Kokusai Bunka Shinkōkai version of the *Manyōshū* gives this translation:

> I shall think of nothing more now.
> To you I have yielded, my dear;
> Upon you my soul leans.
>   (p. 115)

293 (*Kakyō Hyōshiki*; Z 276)
The length of time is conspicuously long; and the dew on the autumn foliage conspicuously meets the eye. These two ideas are bound together in one poem by the word "conspicuous."

294 (*Kakyō Hyōshiki*; Z 277)
There is a variant in the *Manyōshū* (no. 1394) which is given as anonymous.

295 (*Kakyō Hyōshiki*; Z 287)
Similar to *Manyōshū* nos. 1930 and 1274.
Hikitsu contains the word *hiku*, meaning "to draw." Thus the *makura-kotoba* "*azusa* bow."

296 (*Kakyō Hyōshiki*; Z 288)
The song revolves around a pun between *ichishi* (wild strawberry) and *ichishiroku* (clear, evident, conspicuous). "Shall my yearning be open for all to see, like the strawberries which bloom by the roadside? No, I shall yearn secretly, so that no one will know."
Similar to *Manyōshū* nos. 2255 and 2480.

297 (*Kakyō Hyōshiki*; Z 94)
But an almost identical poem is recorded in the *Manyōshū* (no. 2211) as anonymous.
The first two lines are introductory, leading up to the word Tatsuta.
Line 1: a cord tied by a lover as a pledge.
Line 2: a pun on the first part of the word Tatsuta, which also means "stand up" (*tatsu*).

298 (*Kakyō Hyōshiki*; Z 95)

Recorded also in the *Manyōshū* (no. 27) as the work of Emperor Temmu, but in a slightly different version. Based on a pun connecting the adjective *yoshi* (good) with the first part of the word Yoshino.

Mi is a prefix.

299 (*Kakyō Hyōshiki*; *Z* 97)

300 (*Kakyō Hyōshiki*; *Z* 98)
In the *sedōka* form.

301 (*Kakyō Hyōshiki*; *Z* 99)
There is an identical song in the *Manyōshū* recorded as a *hanka* (envoy) for a *chōka* composed by Hitomaro when Prince Naga was hunting.

302 (*Kakyō Hyōshiki*; *Z* 100)
Identical with *Manyōshū* no. 3225.

303 (*Kakyō Hyōshiki*; *Z* 101)
The same poem as *Manyōshū* nos. 34 and 1716, each of which is attributed to a different author.
"How many ages / Have gone by" since this custom began?

304 (*Kakyō Hyōshiki*; *Z* 102)
However, the *Manyōshū* has the same poem (no. 228), which it attributes to Kawabe-no-Miya-hito, who wrote it in grief when he saw the corpse of a maiden by the pine forest of Hime island in 711 A.D.
Hime island is in the land of Settsu.

305 (*Kakyō Hyōshiki*; *Z* 103)
The same song is recorded in the *Manyōshū* (no. 1320) as anonymous.
The first two lines may mean: "Like the pearls hidden under the sea, I too am full of secret devotion which does not reveal itself openly."
Last line: i.e., for the sake of someone else.

306 (*Kakyō Hyōshiki*; *Z* 120)
The first words of the lines are in Japanese *ana kohishi*, or "ah, how dear," the ancient Japanese equivalent of "I love you."

307 (*Kakyō Hyōshiki*; *Z* 144)

308 (*Kakyō Hyōshiki*; *Z* 145)
Contains a rather conspicuous rhyme scheme:

Kasuga-yama	a
Mine kogu fune no	b
Yakushi tera	c
Awaji no shima no	b
Karasuki no hera	c

309 (*Kakyō Hyōshiki*; *Z* 146)
Evidently another nonsense song; I can make no good sense out of it.

310 (*Kakyō Hyōshiki*; *Z* 147)

311 (*Kakyō Hyōshiki*; *Z* 148)

312 (*Kakyō Hyōshiki*; *Z* 149)

The original is far more laconic:

> At the wind's blowing,
> Clouds' silken awnings:
> Mount Tatsuta:
> Radiantly blooming
> Morning-glory flower (flowers?)

313 (*Kakyō Hyōshiki*; *Z* 150)

Finding List

KOJIKI

Traditional number	My number	Traditional number	My number
1	112	31	105
2	4	32	106
3	5	33	107
4	6	34	146
5	7	35	147
6	8	36	148
7	95	37	149
8	12	38	150
9	14	39	177
10	181	40	117
11	169	41	118
12	172	42	109
13	173	43	35
14	174	44	36
15	175	45	37
16	213	46	38
17	214	47	39
18	215	48	96
19	216	49	121
20	34	50	119
21	275	51	246
22	276	52	151
23	242	53	29
24	245	54	277
25	28	55	40
26	220	56	30
27	221	57	31
28	222	58	97
29	223	59	279
30	182	60	280

Traditional number	My number		Traditional number	My number
61	41		104	122
62	11		105	99
63	281		106	231
64	283		107	232
65	42		108	233
66	43		109	234
67	249		110	235
68	250		111	236
69	251		112	266
70	187		113	267
71	188			
72	86		*NIHON SHOKI*	
73	87			
74	88		Traditional number	My number
75	248		1	112
76	252		2	95
77	253		3	1
78	254		4	10
79	47		5	14
80	48		6	13
81	49		7	181
82	255		8	174
83	256		9	169
84	50		10	170
85	2		11	171
86	32		12	175
87	19		13	172
88	33		14	173
89	20		15	116
90	21		16	71
91	22		17	72
92	51		18	242
93	77		19	243
94	52		20	245
95	78		21	107
96	190		22	105
97	79		23	106
98	258		24	113
99	259		25	220
100	53		26	221
101	85		27	182
102	98		28	176
103	114			

THIS WINE OF PEACE, THIS WINE OF LAUGHTER

Traditional number	My number	Traditional number	My number
29	177	72	255
30	178	73	256
31	179	74	257
32	117	75	258
33	118	76	259
34	109	77	110
35	36	78	100
36	37	79	260
37	38	80	261
38	39	81	262
39	121	82	180
40	17	83	90
41	248	84	115
42	246	85	266
43	151	86	267
44	224	87	234
45	225	88	237
46	226	89	238
47	227	90	239
48	228	91	240
49	229	92	54
50	230	93	55
51	278	94	152
52	279	95	153
53	97	96	9
54	280	97	56
55	281	98	154
56	282	99	268
57	283	100	269
58	11	101	270
59	250 (note)	102	101
60	251	103	102
61	189	104	271
62	86	105	273
63	87	106	274
64	254	107	191
65	44	108	58
66	45	109	193
67	46	110	59
68	18	111	60
69	47	112	205
70	19	113	159
71	50	114	160

Traditional number	My number	Traditional number	My number
115	61	122	206
116	161	123	167
117	162	124	3
118	163	125	207
119	164	126	194
120	165	127	208
121	166	128	62